$wing $tate

Money & Politics in Ohio 2012
by JD Adler

ISBN: 978-0692290897

ePCo press
Philadelphia, PA
contact@jdadler.com

Via Twitter September-November 2012

jim rissier @jm111t
** vote for ignorance, vote Romney! ** Mormon and Jehovah's witness are the most ignorant in the USA! **#Christian #gop #tcot #romney

Patriot @angelos_eirene
@EasternOrthodox @OrthodoxRussian No more Muslim, Barack HUSSEIN Obama. No more Muslim President HUSSEIN

Chan4Chan.com @chan4chan_feed Img #211839 Anon> Romney a shame? How much more of a shame could there be than that stupid nig Obama?

Josh Pyromaniac @joshpyro
People I knew from High School are supporting Romney on Facebook. They are all white and poor so I definitely now know they are racist.

Franklin Bartholomew @fgbart3
If I keep watching T.V. I will convince myself that Romney is gonna lose this election,I need to go to Dick Morris's web site to cheer me up

The Right Pundit @therightnewz
Rush: This Nate Silver Guy is the Only Reason Democrats Aren't Jumping off of Bridges Right Now shar.es/cFEEU

Midget @1tallmidget
What do Obama and OJ Simpson have in common? Their both KILLERS. #Benghazi

Investomunity @investomunity
U.S. stocks drifted lower Monday, as investors turned cautious ahead of an uncertain U.S. presidential election. cnnmon.ie/SOhzhv

Ohio Population: 11.5 million, 5.6m male, 5.9m female

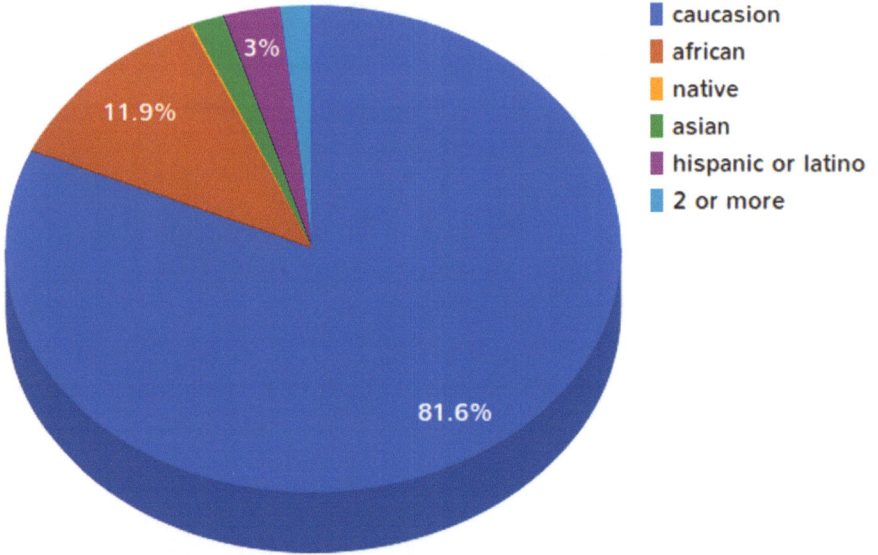

- caucasion
- african
- native
- asian
- hispanic or latino
- 2 or more

3%
11.9%
81.6%

US Population: 309 million, 152m male, 157m female

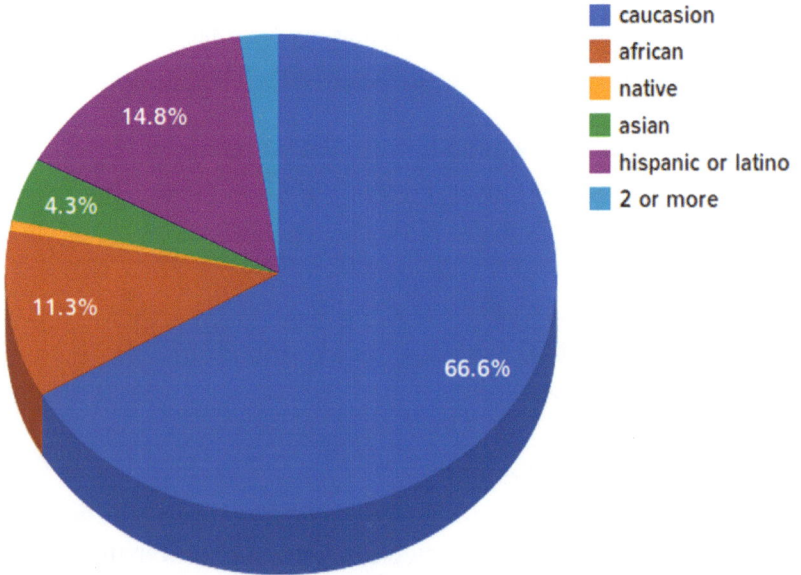

- caucasion
- african
- native
- asian
- hispanic or latino
- 2 or more

14.8%
4.3%
11.3%
66.6%

Source: US Census

Table Of Contents

Ohio, USA

Why is Ohio a swing state? What does it mean to be a swing state? The population of some states vote overwhelming for one political party or the other. Other states are near evenly divided, or have little party loyalty at all. Usually these are states with population distributated across urban and rural communitites. These are the swing states. Each round of elections, it is possible for the dominant political voice to change depending on the mood of the electorate. In the last 5 presidential elections [1], Ohio's results have been almost evenly divided. The slight majority breaking for the national winner. Significantly, in both Clinton and Bush elections, enough people voted for the independent candidate to give the democrat the election; in Ohio and the nation at large.

So, its September 2012, I am unemployed and the election is looming large. The talking heads are claiming several states are in contention, but Ohio and Florida, possibly Virginia, are the only realistic battlegrounds. I decide its time to grow my resume by returning to my roots as a writer. So I head for Ohio to cover the political battle royale for my nation's future.

On stage, President Obama argues for team spirit, while Governor Romney argues for individualism, but that is not the ground battle. In the field, the Democrats are fighting to get every warm body they can find registered and out to the polls, while the Republicans attempt to erect as many hurdles as possible. The result [2]was increased early voting, increased minority voting, and increased youth voting with white turnout decreased for the first time.

Total US votes cast & Net change from 4 years prior
(in thousands)

2012

	Total	Net change
Total	132,948	1,804
White, non-Hispanics	98,041	−2,001
Blacks	17,813	1,680
Asians	3,904	547
Hispanics	11,188	1,443

2008

	Total	Net change
Total	131,144	5,408
White, non-Hispanics	100,042	475
Blacks	16,133	2,117
Asians	3,357	589
Hispanics	9,745	2,158

2004

	Total	Net change
Total	125,736	14,910
White, non-Hispanics	99,567	10,098
Blacks	14,016	1,099
Asians	2,768	723
Hispanics	7,587	1,653

US Census (2)

I traveled Ohio by Greyhound bus. Greyhound is a miopic network of despair. The stations are brightly light with elementary school fluorescents. Seating takes the form of tortorous red metal chairs secured to the floor and each other (in case you were thinking of stealing them for your home decorating needs). The staff is always irritiated to have to speak with you, which I find confusing. At any hour there are disheveled people, smelling of urine, either sleeping or asking for cigarettes. The busses themselves are upholstered by a faded, fleece-like, blue and grey cloth held by years of stains of (thankfully) unknown origin. As the stench from the rear bathroom wafts forward, you are serenaded by at least one patron who doesn't understand the proper vocal level for a cellphone, and that guy whose yelling at nobody. Eventually you will be delivered, close to on time, which is all they really promised.

At first, I stayed at motels and youth hostels, but then I discovered an organization called couchsurfing.org; an international group of thousands who allow people to stay in their homes for free in exchange for being able to do the same. In this way I was able to travel the state for cheap and meet the citizens to whom the politicians were speaking. I met people of a variety of ages and occupations, who took me into their homes, occasionally feeding me, serving as guides and often networking opportunities. All for no remuneration.

What I found were incredibly generous people, mostly annoyed by the presence of the the political machine. Their first response was usually disdain and a desire for the entire subject to go away. When pressed for opinions, they found the Republicans insulting and the Democrats befuddled. Outside of rallies or events, I met no cheerleaders for any party. A feeling that politicians were simply seeking self-aggrandizement and/or profit far outweighed any belief in service. The assumption was that their words were merely pro-forma to gain the votes needed to do whatever they wished. While the television continued to claim Ohio would be tightly contested, I was having trouble finding people willing to say they would vote for Romney. Those saying they would vote for Obama, seemed to be doing so as defensive maneuver against Republican policies. If there was one emotion which held constant, it would be disappointment. The only motive for action; defeat the other guy.

As the Presidential race was flooded with journalists of every stripe, I decided to cover the down-ticket and third party candidates, hoping to capitalize on the political fever and the lack of coverage these races were getting to find papers willing to buy my stories. Though less polished, I found far more passion and policy here. The third party candidates in particular, knowing they had no realistic chance of election, were excited and knowledgeable about their issues. The lack of money which kept them off the stage and prevented garnering American votes, a common rallying point.

Money is the core issue of American political life. Most of the top [100 contributors](#) [3]in every election, give to both parties, often in near equal amounts. This creates a base level for participation far above what any third party or independent can muster on their own. Recent Supreme Court decisions relaxing election finance law will only excerbate that situation.

Money buys ads which results in media coverage. Talking heads cover the front runners, instead of providing new information about alternatives. Between front runners, more money doesn't always equal victory but you can't be a front runner without it. Which means you cannot get elected without joining one of the two political parties and getting supported by the wealthiest people within your constituency. A system political theorists call a plutocracy.

plu·toc·ra·cy noun \plü- 'tä-krə-sē
: government by the richest people
: a country that is ruled by the richest people
: a group of very rich people who have a lot of power
- Merriam Webster

Unfortunately, the combination of the digital age and the recession meant a decline in freelance opportunities. Despite interviewing US Senators and significant state politicians, most of my work only ended up on my blog. From those articles, my notes, and my photos, and my experiences couch surfing, the following is my perspective on Ohio in September/October of 2012, as the election season was coming to a head.

Enjoy.
JD Adler

External Links
[2]https://www.census.gov/prod/2013pubs/p20-568.pdf
[3]https://www.opensecrets.org/orgs/list.php

Cleveland, Ohio
October, 2012

I roll into town on the grim carriage that is Greyhound welcomed by a beautiful, chilly autumn evening. As we left Pittsburgh with the setting sun, a slender, dirty white male of indeterminate age under 40 nervously shifts in his seat, across the row from me, eagerly awaiting lights out. My eye is drawn by his rapid, furtive motions, through the dim light cast by passing marketing and neighboring dome lights. I watch in morbid fascination as he quickly rolls up his sleeve, hurriedly searches his pockets, covertly presses his fist into his arm, head lulls back against the window and then he goes limp, sliding off the seats onto the floor where he remains until we arrive. Please don't vomit right here, is my first thought, as I realize he must have just shot up heroine.

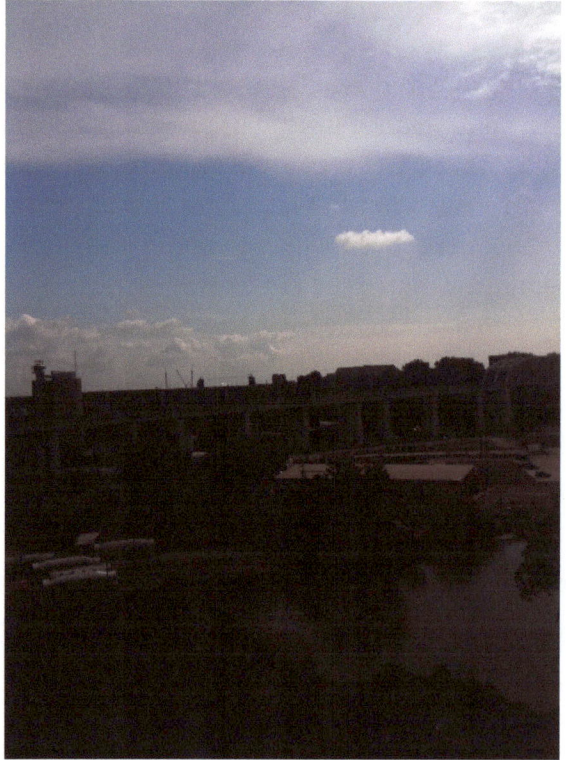

All of my possessions for this adventure are contained in a single backpack resting on the seat between the window and me; 3 pair underwear, 2 pants, 2 long sleeve shirts, 2 short sleeved, 3 pair socks, toothbrush, toothpaste, deodorant, zonegran (epilepsy meds), 16 energy bars, a razor, a bus pass, my ipad, headphones, iphone, a moleskin notebook, a pen, a knife, a flashlight and 5 packs of cigarettes. I have reservations at a youth hostel somewhere in town. With my iphone and the assistance of a public transit driver, I manage to find my way without incident.

The streets of downtown Cleveland are remarkably empty for 10 pm in a major city. Decorated in pastel green and orange trim on white, illuminated by yellow-white street lights, walking from the Greyhound station to the local public transit stop felt like entering one of those touristy bubble scenes of a city. I half expected that, at any moment some giant, fat hand from middle America, extending from a loud, polyester shirt, would shake us and send confetti flying everywhere.

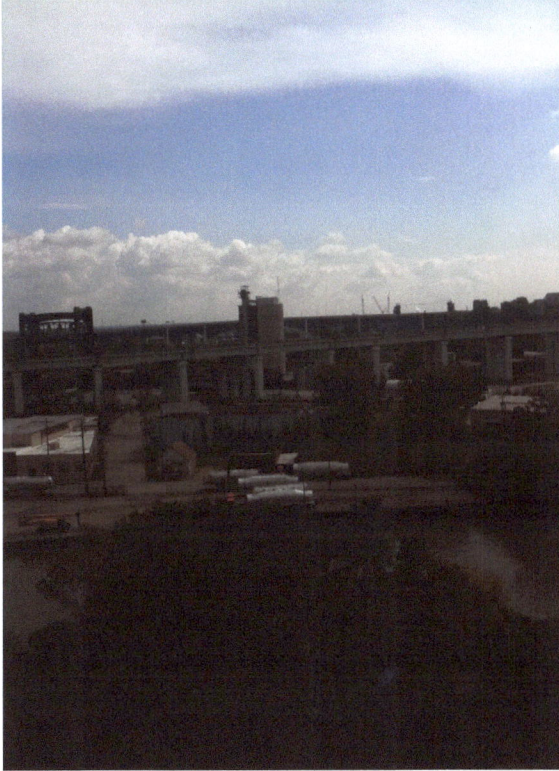

Public transit in Cleveland exists. They have clearly spent time and money insuring the stops blend well into the surrounding scheme. If you only need to travel once per hour, it can be quite helpful. The moderate fall weather was a blessing, as I found myself walking a great deal. During the day, the city itself will surprise with its beauty and activity. Post modern architecture contrasted by large, flourishing parks that surround and punctuate the area. The neighborhoods are lined with trees and rows of 50's era housing. The Cuyahoga River, once a fiery example of industrial pollution that convinced President Nixon to create the EPA, has been turned around into a dingy, grey example of what a city waterway can truly become, complete with the re-emergence of actual water life and the occasional power boat to endanger them.

Walking through Cleveland allows one to see a city in transition. One district is newly renovated and bustling, the next a ghost town of empty warehouses followed by crumbling housing. By the end of an hour walk, you are now in the central business district containing mall shopping, government, and a casino. The regional universities are attempting energy and environment projects on Lake Michigan, but are facing resistance from state politicians who care more about defeating the other team than project outcomes.

The youth hostel I stayed at was a fairly recent addition to the city, in a newly renovated district, providing me cheap housing. Hardwood floors and tables, dusty maps and wifi, minimalist, yet comfortable, design using wood whenever possible, they perfectly captured a mix of styles I can only describe as post-modern rustic. I don't know if that's a thing, but

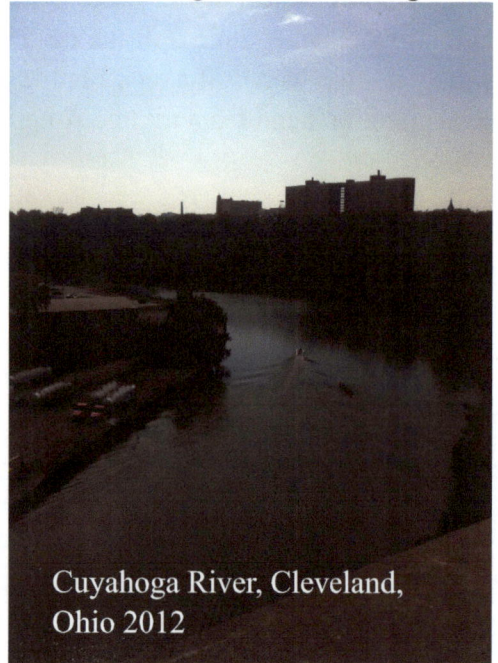

Cuyahoga River, Cleveland, Ohio 2012

that's what I'm calling it. The true benefit of hostels, even more than the price, is the people coming from everywhere on the planet for adventure. They gather, mingle, head off together, and then go their separate ways. During the few days I stayed at this hostel, I met some Swedes, a Dane and a Japanese couple, as well several Americans attempting Kerouac.

A few days in, I had interviewed the county Democrats, attended an early voting event, and attempted to interview the county Republicans. The latter refused to speak with me because I wouldn't provide my questions in advance. I was waiting for responses for my next interview requests, when I was invited to a pot luck dinner held in a local park, by one of the women working/living at the hostel. The pot luck offered several tents and tables and fantastically tasty, unhealthy mid-western food alongside vegetarian stuff that, let's face it, isn't food so much as filler. All set up along the shore of Lake Michigan, offering a fantastic view of the city.

There was not a politician in sight. No one made promises or offered accusations. A group of people had a problem to solve, so they got together, ate and raised money and attention. Everyone was very happy and friendly. When conversation turned to why I was in Ohio, everyone would shake their heads, raise their palms, and declare they had enough of that topic already. These were not uninvolved or uneducated people. They simply had no faith that a political conversation served any purpose, and were tired of the overlong political season.

The woman who invited me, call her "Stella", a tall woman with shoulder length blonde hair that bounces when she bobs her head, ended up getting sidetracked and never showed. Intelligent, slightly flakey, she has one of those infectious smiles, but her eyes beg for a comforting hug. Now living and working in the hostel, as an escape hatch from a boyfriend/ boss relationship with an influential local, she finds all the progress made escaping a wild youth erased, coinciding with a recession. Constantly on the move, Stella is attempting to rebuild her graphic design business despite the attempt by her ex to blacklist her in the local community.

Alone, at this charity pot luck, a young brunette, "Jenny", picks me up. I would later learn I was revenge on her ex, which made me feel used and dirty, but in a good way. Jenny's a cello player, both as a performer and an independent teacher. Thick Jewish curls and a bright round face, with big round eyes, and the kind of wide lower body that's perfect for balancing a large string instrument. We drove back to her house situated

Sen. Sherrod Brown with local Union members at first day of early voting, Cuyahoga County

mid-block in a blue collar, middle class neighborhood. Grassy front yard, two stories, hardwood floors, dimly lit, papers everywhere, a piano dominating the front room, glass panes in the swinging doors between rooms, sunlight filtering through from high windows, I felt like I was entering a movie about a music teacher. It occurred to me that in Philly, she could never have afforded such a large place, in such a nice neighborhood. Clearly the wealth gap was not as severe in Cleveland.

The next day, there was a concert in the postage stamp sized park up the block from the hostel. People wandered in and out while local bands performed awful covers of Led Zeppelin and Nirvana. Children played while their parents rebuffed beggars, and traveling anarchists gathered to trade info on their underground network of campsites and off the book jobs. Later that day I ran into Stella. As I tried to figure out my next destination, she brought up couchsurfing.org.

I had never heard of this before; an international organization of people who offer free places to sleep, in their homes, in exchange for being able to receive the same when they travel. I joined immediately. The site format is familiar: user page, forum, in-site email, rate/comment, ID verify, etc. I was able to post publicly where I would be going, for how long, and ask if anyone could house me, and/or send messages to specific people requesting to crash at specific times. In this way I was able travel Ohio for free, for the rest of the month. I do not know if I could have afforded to complete the trip otherwise.

Cleveland, Ohio

Ohio Congressional Districts
2002-2012

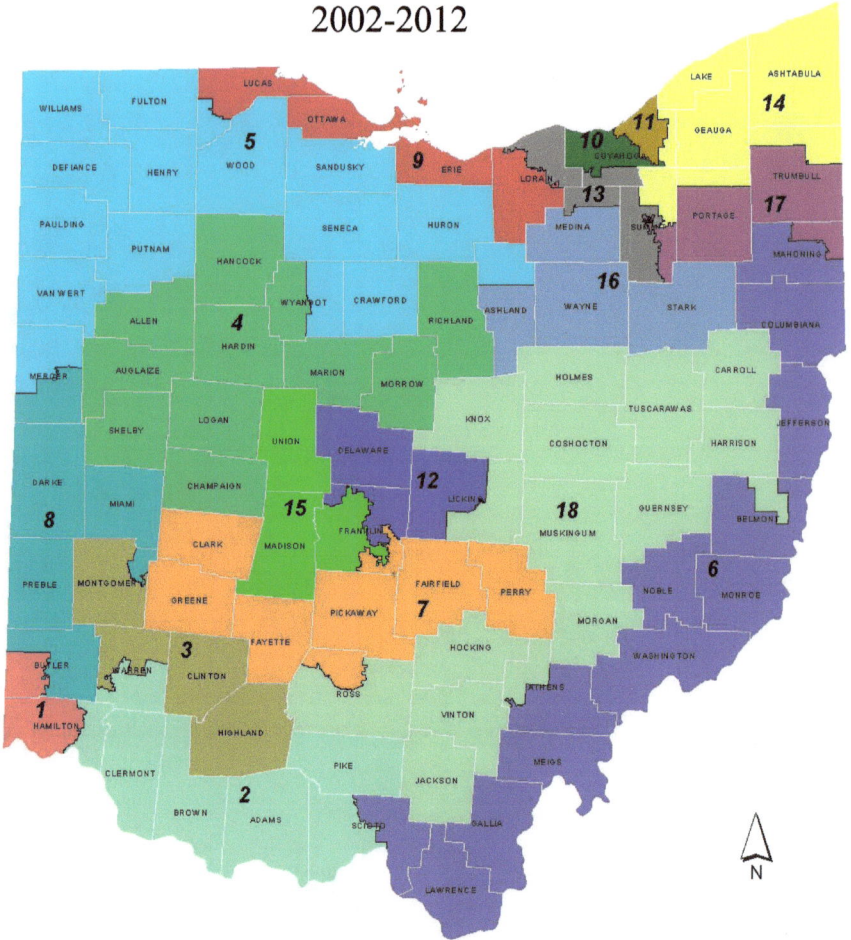

WILLIAMS
FULTON
LUCAS
LAKE
ASHTABULA
14

DEFIANCE
HENRY
WOOD
5
OTTAWA
SANDUSKY
9
ERIE
LORAIN
10
CUYAHOGA
11
GEAUGA
TRUMBULL
17

PAULDING
PUTNAM
SENECA
HURON
MEDINA
13
SUMMIT
PORTAGE
MAHONING

VAN WERT
HANCOCK
WYANDOT
CRAWFORD
RICHLAND
ASHLAND
WAYNE
16
STARK
COLUMBIANA

ALLEN
4
HARDIN
MARION
MORROW
HOLMES
CARROLL
JEFFERSON

MERCER
AUGLAIZE
LOGAN
UNION
DELAWARE
KNOX
COSHOCTON
TUSCARAWAS
HARRISON

SHELBY
CHAMPAIGN
15
12
LICKING
18
MUSKINGUM
GUERNSEY
BELMONT
6

DARKE
MIAMI
CLARK
MADISON
FRANKLIN
FAIRFIELD
PERRY
NOBLE
MONROE

8
MONTGOMERY
GREENE
PICKAWAY
7
MORGAN
WASHINGTON

PREBLE
3
FAYETTE
HOCKING

BUTLER
WARREN
CLINTON
ROSS
ATHENS

1
HAMILTON
HIGHLAND
VINTON

CLERMONT
PIKE
JACKSON
MEIGS

2
BROWN
ADAMS
SCIOTO
GALLIA

LAWRENCE

N

| 0 | 20 | 40 | 60 | 80 | 100 | Miles |

Prepared by:
Northern Ohio Data & Information Service
Maxine Goodman Levin College of Urban Affairs
Cleveland State University
(216) 687-2209
http:\\nodis.csuohio.edu

January 2002 mjs

Source: CSUohio

Ohio Congressional Districts 2012-2022
(As Adopted 2012)

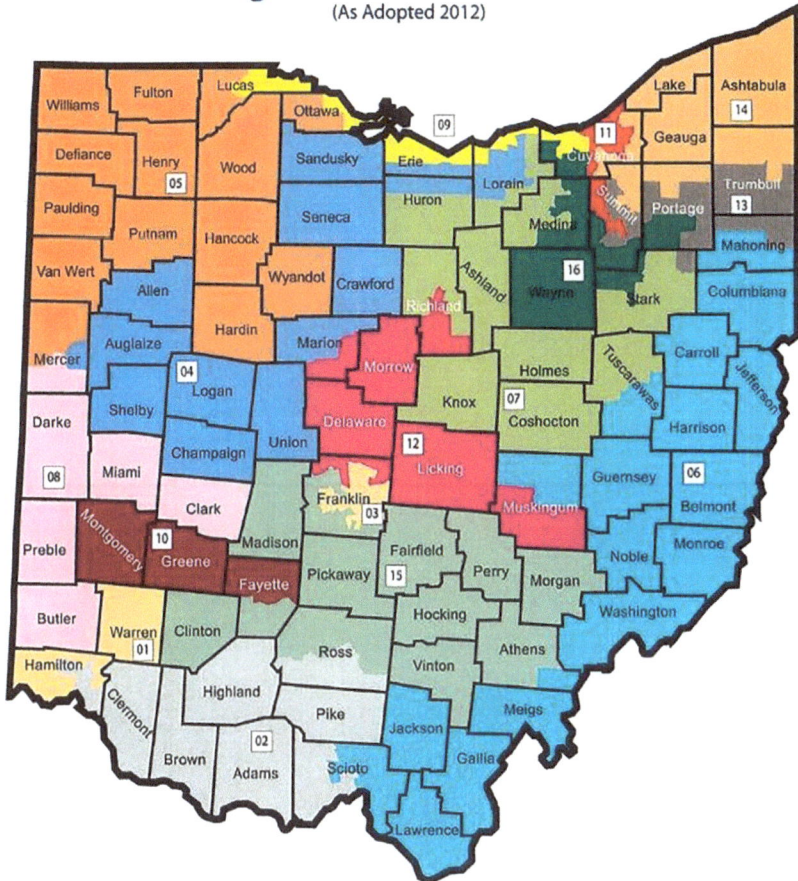

Source: KSUohio

Early Voting in Ohio

Ohio Early Voting Trends 2006 - 2012

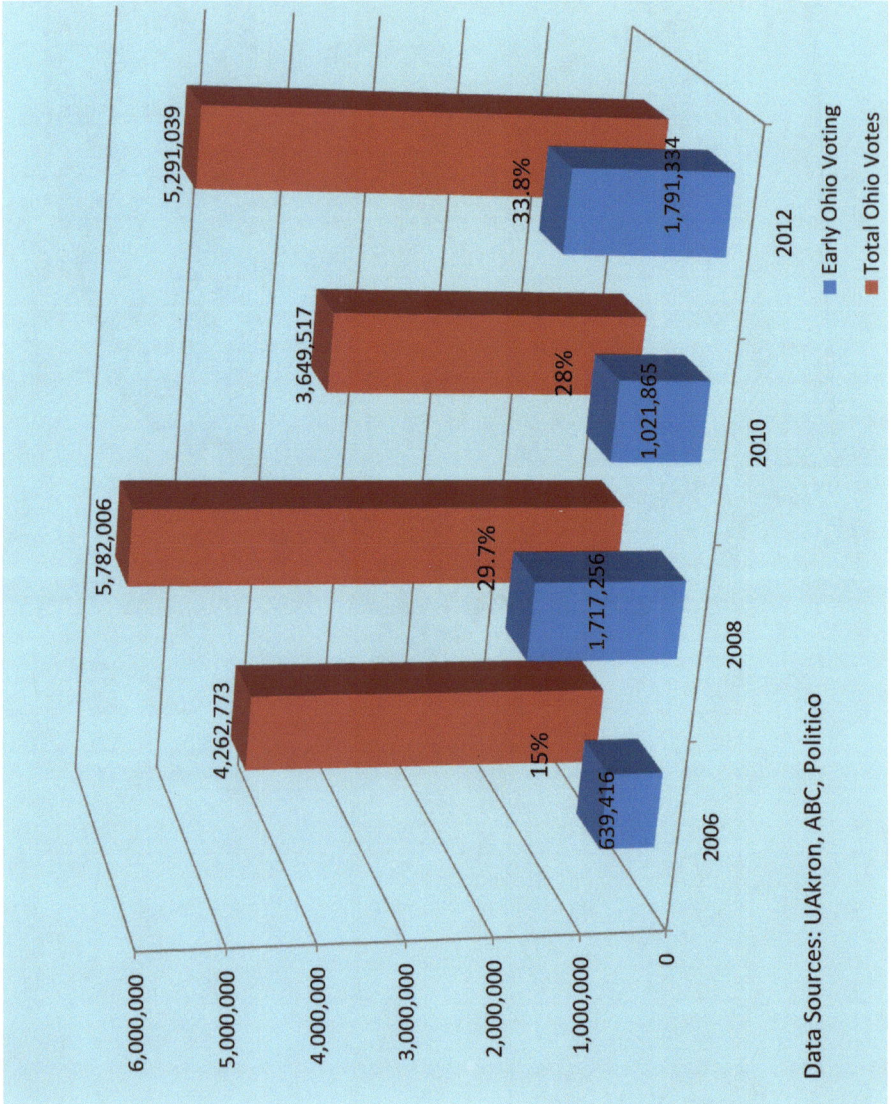

Ohio Early Voting Controversy

October, 17, 2012

In the state of Ohio there has been a great deal of attention brought to the process of early voting this year, and the controversies surrounding the legal battles regarding its implementation. Accusations of racism,

Dennis and Commisioner Lieberman

classism, voter suppression, and slander have been tossed about. At the same time, Ohio has also just undergone a redistricting this year, as required after every census. This has also led to a controversial battle over a ballot issue (#2 in Ohio [2]) designed to amend the state constitution so that, ideally, the process of redistricting would no longer be controlled by the party which won the last election, AKA gerrymandering. Ohio is always a battleground state in national election years due to its near even divide between urban and rural, Democrat and Republican, voters, but the addition of all this election process maneuvering has made this year particularly fascinating for the political wonk.

From the Left

One of the first interviews I did on the subject was with a former election board member from Montgomery County, Ohio; Dennis Lieberman. The reason he is a former member is that he and Tom Ritchie, both Democrats, were fired earlier this year, by the Ohio Secretary of State John Husted, for voting to keep weekend voting open after receiving a directive not to do so, as did every election board in the state. This was neither the first, nor the last, chapter in this story.

As Lieberman tells the story, early voting has been used in the state as a result of the 2004 election cycle which had massive lines that led to people leaving without voting. As a result, 27% of the electorate has been voting early, lines were reduced dramatically, precincts were able to be condensed on election day, and a net $150,000 was saved by the state annually. In 2008 they received 45,000 mail in early votes, 29,000 in person early votes, and 12,000 in the weekend before election day. These details from the past election cycles had already been budgeted and planned for the 2012 election, according to Lieberman.

On the 17th of August the Ohio Secretary of State sent a directive to the election boards informing them to allow Monday through Friday early voting only.

Because 50% of African Americans had been early voting on weekends, often through church groups that bussed them to locations, Lieberman felt obligated to protect that option, and so he voted to accept the directive, plus keep weekend voting. It was a 2-2 vote along party lines on the Montgomery County Board.

The law requires the Secretary of State to break ties. Instead, Husted demanded they rescind the vote or risk being fired. Technically, since they had already adjourned, it would be a violation of the Sunshine Act for them to meet and vote on the issue again. However, a second meeting was held at 2pm, resulting in nothing changing. Over the next several weeks, Lieberman and Ritchie were first suspended and then fired by Secretary Husted for "non-feasance" (failure to perform an act required by law). They are pursuing legal action and await a court appearance on October 23rd.

Lieberman also informed me the Secretary had recently issued a directive that election boards could not contact people about registration form errors, as they had in the past, which would result in their not being registered or able to vote.

I asked Lieberman what he thought the motive for these actions could be. "This is the most deceptively partisan Secretary of State we have ever had. His philosophy seems to be discouraging voting in the name of uniformity. I believe in striving for 100% voter turnout. He's bringing us down to counties that have [only] 1700 people voting. Jim Crow was uniform, but not fair."

From the Right

I have attempted to contact Secretary Husted for comment or interview on several occasions without response. I did, however, have the opportunity to speak with Matt Borges, the Executive Director for the Republican Party of Ohio, recently and we did discuss this issue among others. While the full interview will be published later, excerpts on this subject seem appropriate here.

He offered a very different perspective on these events. Although he had no information on the financial aspect, nor could I find confirmation of Lieberman's numbers, the history regarding lines and the need for relief, and the voting turnout numbers, is undisputed. He informed me the initial proposal to create early voting was a Republican initiative which the Ohio Democrats unanimously voted against. In 2011 a request came to the legislature, from a bipartisan election commission, to reduce the early voting period to 17 days and exclude the weekend before due to concerns over record accuracy on two counts. The concern with the weekend before voting is that the election board does not have the opportunity to log the votes and prevent double votes. The concern with 35 day voting is a "golden week" in which people can register and vote on the same day, leaving no opportunity to verify the registrations. This request was passed by the legislature, in 2012, and then later repealed by Republicans due to the emotions surrounding the issue, according to Borges.

Others [3] view that series of events differently. In 2011, legislation was passed [4] that created the new, limited early voting calendar and a referendum on it, to occur during the 2012 primaries. That repeal [5], which Borges refers to, repealed both the new limits and the referendum, thereby preventing a public statement on the issue.

Executive Director, Republican Party, Ohio

October 22, 2012

Last week I had the opportunity to sit down with Matt Borges, the Executive Director of the Republican Party in Ohio. We discussed his background, the Supreme Court race, the Presidential race, electoral redistricting, and issues surrounding early voting in Ohio.

Matt Borges

Borges has had a long career with the Republican Party. He began working for the RNCC in 1992, and he has worked on the campaigns of VP Cheney, Senator McCain, Ohio state Treasurer Deter(whose staff he also served on), and Ohio Govenor Kasich's inaugural committee.

He has also had some controversy in his career. In 2004, while working for Treasurer Deter,he plead guilty [2] to misdemeanor charges related to inappropriate use of campaign funds in which donations intended for Deter's campaign had been redirected to the county party fund. A plea that was later expunged from his legal record. When I asked Borges about these charges, he ascribed the entire situation to a corrupt prosecutor who was attacking Deter, a potential political adversary. Directing people to "google Cuyahoga County Corruption [3]…worst people you could have the misfortune of coming across." While there appears to be little doubt that there was corruption on the other side, all that seems to affirm is the universality of the corruption rather than absolving him of any particular accusation.

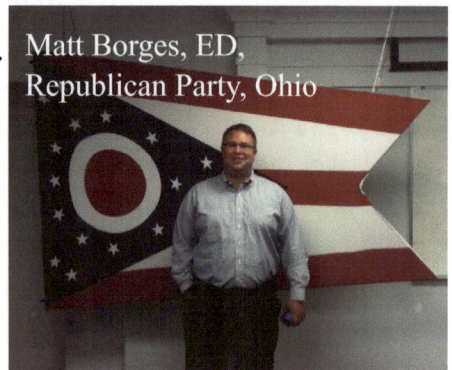

Matt Borges, ED, Republican Party, Ohio

The other issue being slung at Borges is the fact that between his tenure on Kasich's inaugural committee and his current post, he has been employed as a lobbyist [4]. This created consternation among liberals and conservatives alike on two fronts. On the other hand, the Governor has long been an outspoken and visceral critique of lobbyists. On the other, one of the firm's clients, who Borges did some work for, was a Gay Rights organization called Equality Ohio.

To the first issue, Borges admitted the Govenor did not really like his decision to take that job, but the 20+ years they had spent developing a trust between them surpassed any particular job. The second issue is more sticky, because he was taking harsh criticism from the family values base of the party, including calls for his removal, based on his association with Equality Ohio. Borges suggests these people should have taken more time to find out the full story, while conceding he could have handled his communications on the subject better. He describes his participation as minimal. The organization was a client of the firm, his employer assigned him a task, and he did the job. Apparently some people suggested he should have quit on principal, but his principal was supporting his child.

Campaign Strategy

One of Borges' primary jobs is to organize and strategize the state party election plan. With the Romney campaign currently mounting a surge, I asked him if he attributed this to any particular thing. He described the first debate as a "definition shot in the arm. The psychological effect of the polls had been making people nervous." However, the plan is "old school, direct contact". They had been averaging 150-160 thousand doors knocked on per week, which had been increased to 250 thousand in the last two weeks. He stressed the importance of speaking to as many, everyday people as possible. The other key component is coordinating the messages of candidates and surrogates so that they are mentioning each other's names and ideas in their statements, reinforcing concepts for the electorate. (interestingly, this mirrored the strategy discussion I had with the Democrat ED, Nick Martin)

I asked Borges if he was concerned about attrition from the right undermining any swing vote gains, due to Libertarian candidate Gov.

Gary Johnson polling at 10%, and the Ron Paul supporters planning a write in campaign. He dismissed this concept out of hand, arguing that internal polling has Romney polling at 93% among Republicans.

Election Law

As discussed in more detail in this recent article [5] regarding early voting in Ohio, I asked Borges about the recent controversies surrounding early voting and redistricting in Ohio.

The central issues surrounding redistricting and Issue 2 on the ballot, is the idea that whichever party holds a majority in the state assembly after the census is able to control the district map for the next ten years. Borges pointed out that not only have the newspapers described Issues 2 as poorly crafted piece of legislation, but also that for decades minority parties have been wining elections despite gerrymandering. In short he trusts the "integrity of elections" more than a poorly designed "constitutional amendment that we will never be able to undo".

On the early voting issues, Borges described the accusations of voter suppression and attempts to end early voting in general by the Republicans as a mischaracterization of what has been happening. Rather, the Republicans were merely attempting to comply with election committee requests to deal with 2 issues created by early voting: 1) voting the weekend before election day opened the door to double voting because they couldn't verify votes fast enough, and 2) voting a month before allowed for same day registration and voting, the so called "golden week", which allowed for in person fraud because there is no chance to verify the registration. (While numerous reports show in person voter fraud is virtually non existent, registration fraud is a real problem every election cycle.)

Borges also informed me that Republicans repealed this law due to "the emotions" surrounding the issue. In fact, they repealed the early voting laws and the Democrat legislation that required they be put to a public referendum. Leaving only the legislation recently overturned in the courts, that would have allowed early voting only for members of the military. When I asked Borges if he thought It want unfair to allow some citizens to vote but not others, he said he felt, Asa a civilian, members of the military deserved special privilidges.

Confidence

Overall, in terms of strategy, mood of the electorate, and past decisions, Matt Borges is confident and optimistic. He is not arrogant enough to believe he has made no mistakes, but he does feel assured of the course the party is on and foresees victory across the tickets this November.

External Links

[2]
http://www.google.com/url?q=http%3A%2F%2Fwww.enquirer.com%2Feditions%2F2004%2F07%2F28%2Floc_loc1treas.html&sa=D&sntz=1&usg=AFQjCNGtpwhd2easd96zX8VcqHVTQtY2-A
[3]
http://www.google.com/url?q=http%3A%2F%2Fthirdbasepolitics.blogspot.com%2F2012%2F10%2Fed-fitzgerand-just-another-corrupt.html&sa=D&sntz=1&usg=AFQjCNFV0Uy8o8e-rrEELZ_Xe0_FU7DdZA
[4]
http://www.google.com/url?q=http%3A%2F%2Fwww.dispatch.com%2Fcontent%2Fstories%2Flocal%2F2012%2F05%2F23%2Flobbyist-named-new-gop-director.html&sa=D&sntz=1&usg=AFQjCNFtMlO6UbcspphrDWoLiSFZoWIU0g
[5]
http://www.google.com/url?q=http%3A%2F%2Fjdadler.com%2Fohio-early-voting-controversy%2F&sa=D&sntz=1&usg=AFQjCNGzsTVNDwPaoC6ySEnKVzsGfIrPWg

Cuyahoga County Dems
Cleveland, Ohio 9/28/12

This afternoon I met with the Executive Director of the Cuyahogo County Democrats, Nick Martin. Next door to the Crazy Horse tavern, just a stones throw from the Rock-n-Roll hall of fame, an excited crew of volunteers and staff electrified the small office. While phones rang off the hook (okay phones don't really have hooks anymore) and volunteers made calls, campaign managers circulated through, checking in with their director. Though they gratefully acknowledged his support and organizational skills, he would only admit to a minor role in actually putting together their work, "herding cats" as he described it.

Nick Martin

A full time Democrat Party operative, Nick was brought to the county office from the state offices after a house cleaning at the county level a couple of years prior. His job was to refocus the party message and candidate activity to a more unified scheme, alongside the state and national plans. No small job in the second largest Democrat county in the nation, in a state which has just undergone a massive redistricting. Part of Nick's vision for moving the party message forward, is overcoming the "binary outcome" concept of elections wherein everything is either good or bad depending on outcome. He feels it is important to recognize that winning or losing the election does not mean you did everything right or wrong, and it is important to parse the elements for future campaigns.

The Message

"A Fair Shot where everyone Pays a Fair Share and Plays by the Same Rules."

A fairly simple and straightforward statement that the Democrats have been putting forward from the President on down this election cycle. Nick's job is not only to keep all the down-ballot candidates on message, but also to coordinate their activities.

Utilizing "force multiplier" effects by having each candidate speak not only for themselves, but each other as well, the goal is continuous reinforcement in the minds of the electorate. It is hoped that this, combined with the positive influence of the President's campaign, will have a positive influence on the minds of the people of Ohio.

Key Races

Of course every race is important, but the redistricting of Ohio has put several races into stark relief for the Democrats. One example of particular importance to both parties is the Sutton v Renacci race which pits two incumbents against each other. Sutton is of special note to both parties as she was co-sponsor of the "cash for clunkers" bills which helped moved the auto economy in the early days of the recession.

Get out the Vote

Messaging and coordination are all well and good, but in the end it's the votes that matter. Between the confusion of the redistricting and the battle over early voting, the citizens of Ohio have had a series of mixed messages this year. So Democrats have planned early voting events and been mailing out forms for requesting early voter ballots containing sample Democrat ballots. All in a massive effort to insure that the votes they need arrive in the ballot box.

In that same year the Ohio legislature passed law [6], 88-0, allowing for early military voting, to match Federal requirements. This legislation also eliminated early voting in the weekend before election day, per the request from the election commission. The latter of which the Obama Administration is now suing to have invalidated by the courts (update below). If there had been a referendum, this too would have been covered. I asked Borges if there wasn't an injustice to allowing some citizens to vote early but not others. He was adamant that the military deserves special privileges, and as a civilian he had no problem with this.

On whether it was appropriate for the Secretary of State to fire Lieberman and Ritchie, he simply said, "They weren't disagreeing, they broke the law." He was almost equally succinct about the issue of redistricting. "…it's about the integrity of elections. Go back to the 70's and 80's when the …up through the 90's… and you see the opposing party winning elections [despite the gerrymandering]."Resolution

As of Oct. 16, the Supreme Court decided [7]against the Ohio Secretary of State's appeal, and did not overturn the lower Federal court's decision that early voting in Ohio will be allowed the weekend before election day. Secretary Husted said simply, "…the time has come to set aside the issue for this election." Issue # 2 [independent redistricting panel] will be decided on election day, though it has been derided by nearly every newspaper as quixotic and poorly written. Historically, when voters don't fully understand an issue they vote to keep the status quo.

[update: issue #2 was defeated by 63% and the Lieberman case was dropped [8], "Lieberman said Friday that they decided to let the case go because a successful outcome would have involved taxpayer money being awarded to them. He also said they didn't want to work for Secretary of State Jon Husted.]

External Links
[1]
http://www.google.com/url?q=http%3A%2F%2Fjdadler.com%2Fohio-early-voting-controversy%2F&sa=D&sntz=1&usg=AFQjCNGzsTVNDwPaoC6ySEn
KVzsGfIrPWg

[2]
http://www.google.com/url?q=http%3A%2F%2Fballotpedia.org%2FOhi
o_Redistricting_Amendment%2C_Issue_2_(2012)&sa=D&sntz=1&usg
=AFQjCNE_Irm9sodp_SS4lX-mN1goREXWKw
[3]
http://www.google.com/url?q=http%3A%2F%2Fwww.cleveland.com%2
Fopen%2Findex.ssf%2F2012%2F05%2Fohio_house_votes_to_repeal_c
on.html&sa=D&sntz=1&usg=AFQjCNGgMx09-
pKExB8pT4yYwC2IBHoQ7w
[4]
http://www.google.com/url?q=http%3A%2F%2Fwww.legislature.state.o
h.us%2Fanalyses.cfm%3FID%3D129_HB_194%26ACT%3DAs%2520
Enrolled&sa=D&sntz=1&usg=AFQjCNGbAEKVvib6GnveK7BVRNr_
GwU5Ww
[5]
http://www.google.com/url?q=http%3A%2F%2Fwww.lsc.state.oh.us%2
Fanalyses129%2F12-sb295-
129.pdf&sa=D&sntz=1&usg=AFQjCNEoD5jmy3ufSbq-
BQ63FMLUdIg8mw
[6]
http://www.google.com/url?q=http%3A%2F%2Fwww.legislature.state.o
h.us%2Fanalyses.cfm%3FID%3D129_HB_224%26ACT%3DAs%2520
Enrolled&sa=D&sntz=1&usg=AFQjCNFB534-UOcr6a0xd4YZx9kxhS-
_Ag
[7]
http://www.google.com/url?q=http%3A%2F%2Fwww.bloomberg.com%
2Fnews%2F2012-10-16%2Fohio-early-voting-cleared-by-high-court-in-
obama-
victory.html&sa=D&sntz=1&usg=AFQjCNGXRq6HX0dILaKf43tKgSI
nIob35Q
[8]
http://www.google.com/url?q=http%3A%2F%2Fwww.cantonrep.com%
2Fx1107411934%2FFired-Dems-drop-suit-against-Ohio-elections-
chief&sa=D&sntz=1&usg=AFQjCNEA25bO-GwVZ5wo8hglV7-
aiOShuA

Swing State Voting Machines
October 26, 2012

History

1st Day Early Voting, Ohio

In 2000, 2004 and 2008 voting irregularities infamously brought question to the integrity of the American election process. After the 2000 election, Clinton Curtis, a former programmer for Diebold, testified before Congress [2] that he had been asked by his employer and Republicans from the the Florida state government to write software that would flip votes. In 2004 there were also questions raised by the fact that exit polls in no way reflected the returns shown from the ballots box, although it turned out upon review, such as this Salon article [3], that had more to do with poor polling methodology. In 2008 accusations of voter fraud were rampant, including some legitimate cases [4] that actually led to convictions. As a result, many changes have been made to the systems in the intervening years. We have seen a proliferation of voter ID laws, though focused on in-person voting rather than absentee and registration fraud, which were the actual subject of the criminal cases. The news agencies have altered their reporting to reflect the more accurate exit polling methods. And, for the most part, voting machines have been upgraded.

This Election Cycle

There are four states which have been listed as potential "swing states"; Ohio, Florida, Virginia, and sometimes Colorado. Three of these states are now using either DRE [5] or OS [6] voting machines. Florida, however, continues to use the ES&S (formerly owned by Diebold) GEMS system [7]. All of these systems, due to federal requirements, now utilize a combination of paper and electronic voting records. The

ES&S GEMS systems, however, have been criticized on multiple fronts for the system failings.

Among the two most damning of these critiques are the research paper by Ryan and Hoke, [8] which describes the system architecture as prone to result error, and this video [9]demonstrating how easy it was to hack the GEMS system.

Since 2002 there have been election monitors in the United States from European organization called the Organization for Security and Cooperation in Europe or OSCE. Their mission is to observe a sample set of precincts around the nation and then report their findings to the American people. As they describe on their website [10].

In line with ODIHR's methodology for limited election observation, the mission will not carry out systematic or comprehensive observation of the voting, counting, and tabulation on election day. Mission members will, however, visit a number of polling stations across the country to follow election day procedures.

A statement of preliminary findings and conclusions will be issued and presented to the public on the day after the election. A final report on the observation of the entire electoral process will be published approximately two months after the completion of the election process.

Targets of Opportunity

Election fraud of this type requires access, which is hypothetically attainable. It also requires proper mathematical calculations so that your falsified results appear to be within the margin of error, otherwise alarms will be raised. This means high voter turnout on the opposing side can defeat the fraud. It also requires that any reviewable record, such as a paper copy, can either be destroyed or also altered. While these are certainly attainable objectives, it requires a great deal of foresight, coordination, and post election solidarity among political operatives not exactly known for their mission organization skills.

If there were to be fraud involving falsification of results in this election cycle, the most likely target would be Florida. As a swing state, the results are expected to be close. The machines are known to be vulnerable to hacking, and any suspect could defend themselves by pointing to the fact those machines are also known to be error prone.

On the other hand, both parties and independent observes will be looking for this sort of action, this year more than ever before. A fact that would make career criminals nervous, let alone a political opportunist. It is entirely possible that this may be the most honest election day we have ever witnessed. Then again it may rain gold nuggets and chocolate.

External Links

[1]
http://www.google.com/url?q=http%3A%2F%2Fjdadler.com%2Fswing-state-voting-machines-2012%2F&sa=D&sntz=1&usg=AFQjCNEeK9cePwbB0u13Id8YQM7Ac78x5Q

[2]
https://www.youtube.com/watch?v=JEzY2tnwExs&feature=youtube_gdata_player

[3]
http://www.google.com/url?q=http%3A%2F%2Fwww.salon.com%2F2006%2F06%2F03%2Fkennedy_39%2F&sa=D&sntz=1&usg=AFQjCNFTH1jdmykSxTDTimFXtiOVV0TShg

[4]
http://www.google.com/url?q=http%3A%2F%2Fwww.washingtonpost.com%2Fblogs%2Fvirginia-politics%2Fpost%2Fdozens-charged-with-election-fraud-in-va-in-connection-with-the-2008-election%2F2012%2F04%2F24%2FgIQAkqwueT_blog.html&sa=D&sntz=1&usg=AFQjCNFYn5bp8SWznUhDIc8JiIvFj58slg

[5]
http://www.google.com/url?q=http%3A%2F%2Fen.wikipedia.org%2Fwiki%2FDRE_voting_machine&sa=D&sntz=1&usg=AFQjCNFjxb2ckXaxRsykC1F6H_seotHatg

[6]

http://www.google.com/url?q=http%3A%2F%2Fen.wikipedia.org%2Fw
iki%2FOptical_scan_voting_system&sa=D&sntz=1&usg=AFQjCNFXU
_m--7XB6F40QEXkaLk5xmyEYw

[7]
http://www.google.com/url?q=http%3A%2F%2Felection.dos.state.fl.us
%2Fvoting-
systems%2Fpdf%2FEVS_4030_Ltr_to_SOE_092512.pdf&sa=D&sntz=
1&usg=AFQjCNFRImBimza_SiLrVUGIx9GP_C_EFg

[8]
https://www.google.com/url?q=https%3A%2F%2Fwww.usenix.org%2Fl
egacy%2Fevent%2Fevt07%2Ftech%2Ffull_papers%2Fryan%2Fryan.pd
f&sa=D&sntz=1&usg=AFQjCNHOLds-
Yxqh2ueABYxWmHnyt3RvMA

[9] https://www.youtube.com/watch?v=FbuwbkqAe_A

[10]
http://www.google.com/url?q=http%3A%2F%2Fwww.osce.org%2Fodih
r%2Felections%2F95107&sa=D&sntz=1&usg=AFQjCNGoGPcEjgGO
WqpF3ufnD5HAympkcA

Early Voting Ohio

October 2, 2012

Cleveland, Ohio

US Sen. Sherrod Brown

On a rainy evening in Cuyahoga County citizens gathered with their state and federal senators to camp out for the night before the first day of early voting in Ohio.

Sponsored by state Senator Turner, Sleep Out the Vote was attended by US Senator Sherrod Brown, Cleveland Mayor Jackson, and candidates for local offices, Democrats all. As crowds cheered, each candidate took to the proverbial soapbox and delivered a raucous call to get out the vote in support of President Obama and a "fair playing field". No one more rousing than Turner.

Upstaging even Sen. Brown with her impassioned vow not to let "some backwards Republicans stop us from exercising our right to vote!" the crowd's growing passion was palpable. Brown joked about his misfortune having to follow such a gifted orator. However, this did not prevent him from delivering his own sermon on the need to support the continued efforts of the Democrats on education, health care, and jobs, which drew an impromptu chant of "six more years" from the less than independent audience.

As the night wore on, the rain increased, and the group decreased, but Sen Turner and the faithful stayed the night, making their stand for democracy and voting rights, regardless the conditions.

When asked about the incongruous positions between the Republicans and Democrats on early voting in Ohio, Turner jumped at the opportunity to lay out the facts. "In the rural areas they didn't try and stop early voting, just in the urban areas, where blacks and university students, people who voted heavily for Obama last time, live. This happens at the Board of Elections level. There's two Democrats and two Republicans, by law, and ties are broken by the Republican Secretary of State. She said she voted against early voting because of the tax costs. But there is a cost to denying voting, we have a moral and legal obligation."

Speak with the state senator about any issue and you will get a well argued, liberal case. Speak to her about voting rights or education and you will hear a stirring diatribe on the moral role of government in the lives of the people it serves. "You can't run government like a business, it isn't based on profit motive, it's motive is service!"
When asked how government can deal with the apparent contrary momentums of low revenue during a recession and the Keynesian policy of more investment, Turner replied that the only way to increase the tax base was to get people back to work through educating and infrastructure projects. She then pointed to the lower unemployment rate and current half billion surplus sitting in Ohio's rainy day fund as a result of state and federal investment in those very things. Capping her argument off with, "…trickle down doesn't work!"

State Sen. Nina Turner

Early Voting Sleepout

Via Twitter September -November 2012

Kevin Clark @kcshaddex
Phone poll asked me today if the election was today who I'd vote for, Obama or Romney, I said protest vote, write in Ron Paul.

Roger B @rogerbiles
@NewsNinja2012 @newsninja2012 And Dick Morris polls has Romney leading in 10 of the 12 battle ground states above the 4 point mark!

Derek Gendvil @dgendvil
Daily Kos: Nate Silver: Obama has a 71.6% Chance of Winning the Election dailykos.com/story/2012/08/... via@dailykos

Kate McKinnon @katemckinnon
@JohnWDean @AlanColmes I am encouraged by Nate Silver's forecast. And of course by old men cursing at chairs.

Bobsacto @bobsacto
You won't hear Obama or Romney talk about it but Aug deadliest month this year for NATO in Afghanistan How many more have to be killed?

Jessie Kruger @jessierkay
Seriously every commercial on my pandora lately has either been about Obama or Romney. #sickofit#stfualready

Brandon @wildmanbs
43% certain vote Romney and 42% certain vote Obama...15% are either uncommitted or open to changing their minds! #TCOT rasmussenreports.com/public_content...

Lady Gaga @ladygaga
Did anybody else hear Romney's mic feedback after Obama said "you wouldn't have taken such a sketchy deal, and neither should you" *awkward*

Commentary Magazine @commentary
Unlike analysis of sports & poker — fields Nate Silver is an master in — political polling is more art than science.goo.gl/OV7ba

Dayton, Ohio
October, 2012

My first Couch Surfing host was William Bagwell. They could not ask for a better ambassador. An incredibly generous host, he drove me to and from the bus, around town, cooked for me, and provided entertainment in the form of stories and balloon animals. With a bushy

white beard and hair to match, and a genuine smile anytime of the day or night, William reminds me of my Uncle Sheldon, who was always testing the kids with riddles, puzzles and/or minor magic tricks. They both served in the US Navy, so maybe it has something to do with all that time at sea.

Living on a beautiful, half acre property just outside of Dayton, William's two-story home was filled with hard wood floors and furniture, and memorabilia of his children. We had to reconnect his television so I could watch the debates. An old school, floor model set into a wooden box. Though obviously a replica since it included cable

hook-ups, it still clearly pre-dated the turn of this century. William, a man well versed in a variety of topics from the bizarre to the banal, had no interest in politics. He fully grasped the issues, and I wouldn't call him apathetic, exactly. When questioned, his views were mostly left of center. It was just that he had reached a point where, like his disconnected TV, experience had taught him most of what the system offered was garbage.

I had the opportunity to interview local Democrats, at a local pub hosting an afternoon fundraiser. A traditional sports pub, wood paneling around two rooms divided by a half wall into bar room and seating area, neon signs and TVs secured the high ground and a handful of regulars held court at the bar. Having arrived early, I decided to instigate a political conversation.

A Romney supporter at the bar, call him Eric, soon found himself being lambasted as a racist by his neighbor, although he made no comments to suggest feelings one way or another on the topic. When I pressed for a particular reason he disliked Obama politically, he simply shrugged and said "he hasn't done anything in two years but run for office."

An avid, if somewhat intoxicated, Obama supporter, call him Mike, had been praising a local candidate for the House as a good business women, Eric asked why he didn't support Romney on those grounds. Which lead to a heated diatribe on the villainy of Bain capital, "I guarantee there wasn't one new job created by Romney, he just gutted companies and kept the money!" Eric turned around and pointed out the irony of Mike supporting the local Dem because she was good at business, but then supporting Obama against Romney where the roles were reversed, suggesting the only criteria Mike actually cared about was party allegiance.

The worst part of this whole exchange is that neither of them was correct. Obama had numerous accomplishments in the past two years, such as passage of the veterans' jobs bill, and hadn't begun campaigning seriously until June. Bain capital had, in fact, created numerous jobs at places like Staples. For the last year the media has been flooded with political campaign news, biased in one direction or the other, about these very things. Yet, for the average citizen, confusion and misinformation remained the norm.

Later I spoke to the tavern owner, host of the Democrat Part event taking place there, about the President's tax plan. I pointed out he intended to raise taxes on small business earning more than $250k per year, and wanted to know if that would affect him. He chuckled and said that didn't matter. His business, like all small business, shows little or no profit because he pays himself a salary and rent, and adjusts those amounts to compensate for any changes in revenue. So no matter whose tax plan is in place, neither GM nor small ops like his would be paying any taxes; according to him. Therefore any discussion of business tax is fruitless; it all falls onto the income and capital gains tax systems.

I found myself walking away from this conversation wondering why we bother with a process where everyone is sure they are right, even though no two people seem to agree on the same facts.

View from the Greyhound outside Dayton, Ohio

Via Twitter September-November 2012

Matthew Vadum @vadum
Obama is selling at 67.7 on Intrade, reflecting either bettors' doubts Romney can win OH or mass Obama-zombification. #tcot #p2 #ocra

sid.kangaroo @sid_pass
Christians Will Empower A Romney Landslide : Personal Liberty Digest™ fb.me/1tR31cjpj

Erin Waldschmidt @erinjac
I hate being a swing state. I'm just trying to watch GMA & eat my cheerios & there were 6 consecutive political commercials. C'mon man.

Daniel Tyler @danielt3006
Gingrich Urges Voters to Reject Obama Over Benghazi fb.me/1mWTVG9Eq

RedditTop @reddittop
Press Wakes Up to Romney's Lies, Says There's 'no excuse' for 'astonishingly misleading' Jeep Adreddit.com/r/politics/com...

CowboysForLife @salutethestar
People who love Obama go ahead I'm not voting for him in 2012 or Romney its crazy to pick the lesser of two evils #YeahISaidIt

Leder Hals @lederhals
Obama blasts Romney's proposed tax cuts - usat.ly/Oop2ky or... They wil help employ the middle class. We know Obama is no fan of jobs

Ed Schultz @edshow
President Obama in Ohio: "How many of you want to pay another $2,000 to give people like Mitt Romney or me another tax cut?"

THE LIGHTWERKERZ @tymajestic
THE ETS OR ALIENS ARE WATCHING THIS ELECTION, TO SEE IF WE MATURED IN OUR CHOICE TO GO FORWARD GREEN ENERGY OBAMA or BIG OIL ROMNEY #ufos

Race for the US Presidency

Money, Ideas and Lies.

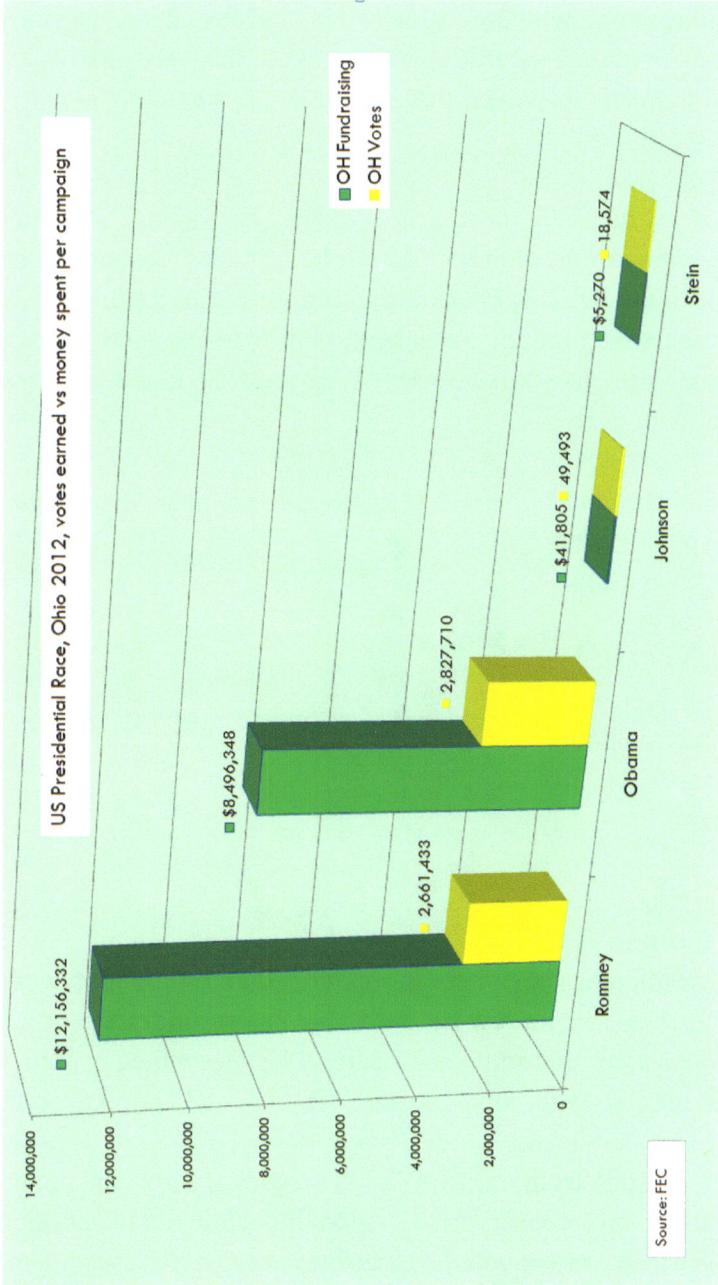

US Presidential Race, Ohio 2012, votes earned vs money spent per campaign

- OH Fundraising
- OH Votes

$12,156,332

$8,496,348

2,827,710

2,661,433

$41,805 49,493

$5,270 18,574

Romney

Obama

Johnson

Stein

14,000,000
12,000,000
10,000,000
8,000,000
6,000,000
4,000,000
2,000,000
0

Source: FEC

Swing and a Pres, the presence of swing votes in politics

Sept. 14, 2012

It is a common meme in modern Presidential politics that there are certain states upon which elections swing because the electorate could vote for one party or the other, while most of the states are politically locked into place. However, this phenomenon is actually new to American politics.

Source [2]

If you review these charts at uselectionatlas.org [3] and click on the election years in the column to your left, it quickly becomes apparent that prior to the 1992 elections the swing state concept did not exist. If one considers the modern era as beginning with President Eisenhower, then in the thirty six years between 1952 and1988 every victorious president won over 420 electoral votes and greater than 50% of the popular vote. This also coincides with the longest period of sustained growth for the middle class in both industry and agriculture.

Average Annual Change in Mean Family Income, 1950-2010, by Quintile and for the Top 5 Percent

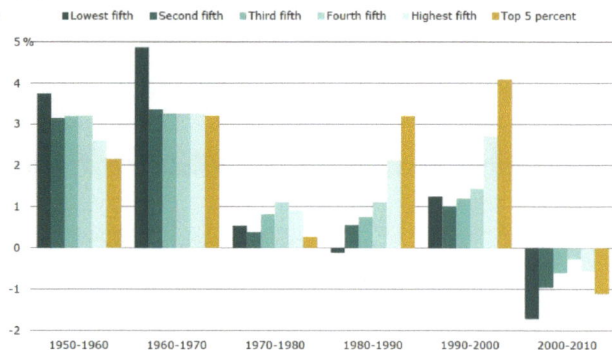

■Lowest fifth ■Second fifth ■Third fifth ■Fourth fifth ■Highest fifth ■Top 5 percent

Since the first Clinton election in 1992, the nation has been both more divided and static in its voting tendencies, with only a few states in play. Interestingly, the primary swing states are in the south and heartland, states which contain both rural and urban populations. Florida, Virginia, and Ohio are considered this years primary swing states. However, if you look at these county by county [4]results from the 2000-2008 elections, it appears the majority of the nation votes conservative, regionally, while the fewer but more populous urban centers vote progressive.

Most striking about these numbers is the close popular vote numbers, as opposed to prior to the swing state era. Bush Sr. had the low number at 53% in 1988, until he was defeated by Clinton with only 43%. Bush jr. would barely break 50% when he was reelected in 2004, and Obama managed to garner 52% in a 2008 election noted for its high voter turnout.

The intended purpose of the electoral college was two-fold. It provided those founders who did not entirely trust the masses to choose wisely, a check through the electors, and it created balance between large and small states so they had near equal influence. But in the modern scenario a few states, possibly counties, have more influence than all others. If we were to abandon the electoral college in favor of the popular vote, then about 5-10% of the population, which has bounced back and forth in recent elections, would settle the philosophical stalemate for all. Is that better or simply rearranging deck chairs on the Titanic?

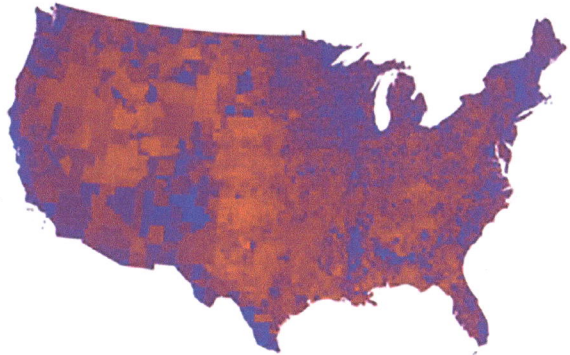

County by County 2008

Some argue that the problem is a two party system which forces a multitude of views into a false polarity. Others suggest that the media should be blamed for feeding the extremes in the hunt for ratings. While there is truth behind these criticisms, ultimately it exists because our nation is divided between a conservative rural culture and a liberal urban culture, each possessing a different perspective on federalist capitalism. While liberals believe government should be used as a tool of public will, conservatives see government as necessary evil which should be limited to the minimum required. The gap between these two subcultures widened by the social and technological changes of the last forty years. This is most difficult in the economic arena because the two views are incompatible. It is very difficult to find an ethical compromise between the laissez faire and Keynesian schools of thought; you cannot have both an unregulated and managed market at the same time. The supply side theory further complicates the issue because it markets itself as laissez faire when in practice it is inverted Keynes, supporting the supplier instead of the consumer.

Whoever wins this next election will have the opportunity to prove their economic theory correct. Should the economy turn around in the next four years, in a manner which can be sustained for an extended period, they should be able to sway enough of this map to set the course through the mid century. Should we continue to languish economically, it is likely the electoral map will remain equally divided until someone does prove themselves.

Perhaps if our leaders addressed the fact that our nation is so clearly divided and entrenched into two camps, instead of getting into the trench warfare, we could make some progress towards uniting.

External Links
[2]
http://www.google.com/url?q=http%3A%2F%2Fcdn.theatlantic.com%2Fstatic%2Fmt%2Fassets%2Fbusiness%2Fassets_c%2F2012%2F08%2FPew_History_Middle_Class_Families_Income_History-96949.php&sa=D&sntz=1&usg=AFQjCNH-TnzqhheRraCqpwernfg4z2WVcA
[3]
http://www.google.com/url?q=http%3A%2F%2Fuselectionatlas.org%2FRESULTS%2F&sa=D&sntz=1&usg=AFQjCNH_7zalJbHN4pEIit3ZA2dR9mJInw
[4]
http://www.google.com/url?q=http%3A%2F%2Fwww.outsidethebeltway.com%2F2008_election_county-by-county%2F&sa=D&sntz=1&usg=AFQjCNH0bnZIpe4N7eFlisHqYUKFn7FjLg

Romney and the Party of Irony
September 1, 2012

Watching the speeches at the Republican convention, I was struck over and over by the disconnect between their beliefs and their plans. If this were a script, the deep interwoven themes building over the course of the 3 nights standing in direct opposition to their proposals would be considered a brilliant work of dramatic irony. As a political platform, it can only be viewed as offensively cynical and opportunistic hypocrisy.

Opportunity/Individualism

If there was 1 theme which ran throughout the convention it was the family history of poor, legal immigrant to successful child/grandchild through independant hard work and education. Every politician regaled us with dramatic nostalgia of their relatives coming to America seeking opportunity and building, through hard work and perseverance, a better life for their children. We are reminded that it was American freedom and opportunity that made this possible for the immigrant, and education that made it possible for their children. All while mocking, out of context and inaccurately, the President's "you didn't build that!" line.

The one thing he [grandfather] wanted me to remember, "You can do anything you want because you are an American."- Sen. Marco Rubio

The great irony here is that the very thing they are describing is the subject of that quote. The opportunity, freedom and education which was unavailable in their family's nation of origin, we built, together, here. The infrastructure, the schools, and the Constitution which secure liberty and produce equal opportunity are the result of "We the people" organizing and developing for common benefit. When Republicans point to immigrants from around the world seeking a better life in America as evidence of our exceptionalism, it is the environment these systems create which they are describing. Yet their entire plan serves to undermine these systems. Which creates exactly the opposite atmosphere from the one their immigrant ancestors enjoyed

Morality

Before every single speaker asked God Almighty to bless the USA, they explained why the values which come from God are responsible for our exceptionalism. We heard about the importance of love, family, integrity, hard work, and charity. Repeatedly, especially by the candidates, we are reminded that our character is demonstrated by how we treat "the least of us."

This administration hasn't passed a budget in 3 years, what does that say about their morals?- Gov. Mike Huckabee

Yet their plans for salvaging our budget rely upon cutting entitlements, welfare, and programs which serve the middle class. They argue that choosing to donate is moral, while being forced to through taxes is tyranny. However, we know from history that voluntary charity does not cover all of the need and suffering. So why are private non-profit charities, that can't do the whole job, acceptable, but the government we all own getting the job done, not acceptable? How is it moral to be more concerned about the label on the institution than the job it accomplishes?

Education

Education reform, as a concept, is almost universally accepted as an immediate need. The Republicans are proposing that a school voucher program, which has been received favorably in areas where it has been tried, combined with ending teacher tenure is the answer. Arguing that choice and opportunity are American values and people should not be trapped by their zip code, Ryan and Romney both harkened back to the value of their own, and their family's, education as they promoted this plan.

When it comes to the school your child will attend, every parent should have a choice, and every child should have a chance.- Gov. Mitt Romney, (R) Pres. Nominee

Yet their immigrant relatives would not have had access to the public schools they praise under their plan. The current generation, those left behind in the poor zip code once the "good choices" have filled up, will find themselves even more disadvantaged and ghettoized than before. By taking the best students and accompanying funds out of the neighborhood, you guarantee that neighborhood will remain impoverished and desperate. Creating the very situation their ancestors fled when seeking opportunity and justice in America.

Small Government

The longstanding belief of the conservative movement that the best government is no government, was reaffirmed throughout the week. The idea that both liberty and opportunity are infringed by government regulations, taxes, and programs, regardless of the good intentions, was hammered home over and over.

And fifth, we will champion small businesses, America's engine of job growth. That means reducing taxes on business, not raising them. It means simplifying and modernizing the regulations that hurt small business the most. And it means that we must rein in the skyrocketing cost of healthcare by repealing and replacing Obamacare.- Gov. Mitt Romney, (R) Pres. Nominee

Yet somehow when it comes to voting, health care decisions, and foreign policy, government intervention is precisely what is needed. They want government IDs required to be able to vote, though they opposed earlier pushes for a national ID. They want the government to serve as intermediary between a woman and her doctor when health care decisions are made. On the foreign stage, they call the President weak for not violating international law and interfering in the internal affairs of other nations, Romney promising he would not just talk.

This last is the most dangerous, if least surprising. Essentially reassuring the NeoCons and military industrial complex that there would be a return to the Cowboy Diplomacy that so enriched them at the expense of everyone else. With no other indication of how Romney intends to provide the 12 million jobs he promised, perhaps we are seeing the beginnings of his job plan, another middle east war with either Syria or Iran, or both, and possibly a return to the cold war with Russia.

In his first TV interview as president, he said we should talk to Iran. We're still talking, and Iran's centrifuges are still spinning.- Gov. Mitt Romney, (R) Pres. Nominee

Leadership/Integrity

Accompanied by nearly every critique of the President over the week, was the reminder that this was an example of a failure of leadership, and the promise that Romney will do better. A key part of doing better, according to Paul Ryan, is being honest with the people and making hard choices.

We will not duck the tough issues, we will lead.

We will not spend four years blaming others, we will take responsibility.

We will not try to replace our founding principles, we will apply our founding principles.- Rep. Paul Ryan (R) VP Nominee

Which leads to the most stunning comparison of the 2 candidates. Politifact [2] lists 190 campaign promises kept by Obama, and 83 broken. This is sharply contrasted by the numerous videos [3] of Mitt Romney taking both sides of the issue on abortion, health insurance, immigration, public education, and taxes.

Do these Republicans really want a debate on integrity, or are they simply being ironic?

External Links

[1]
http://www.google.com/url?q=http%3A%2F%2Fjdadler.com%2Fthe-
party-of-
irony%2F&sa=D&sntz=1&usg=AFQjCNF7_sYj49oo3VgyrkqcXEpgzp
VAog
[2]
http://www.google.com/url?q=http%3A%2F%2Fwww.politifact.com%2
Ftruth-o-
meter%2Fpromises%2Fobameter%2F&sa=D&sntz=1&usg=AFQjCNH
P4OdHLZbmXokKKM8rnrOE6IFqag
[3] https://www.youtube.com/watch?v=K9njHHyRI7g

Paul Ryan, NeoCons, TeaParty, and Libertarians
August 30, 2012

The 2nd night of the Republican Convention was focused on presenting the core themes for the GOP campaign message.

- American exceptionalism is sourced in "free people and free markets" which are best protected by limiting government
- Business provided for roads, roads didn't provide for business
- America needs to lead in the free world by using our military supremacy to support revolutions, stop slaughters, and leverage negotiations
- Budget solutions through program cuts, economic solutions through tax cuts and regulation cuts
- Medicare reform is a debate they can win
- Repeal Obamacare
- President Obama is a weak leader who "believes in a government where everything is free but us." (Paul Ryan)
- Slogans: Stand Up, We Can Do This, Todos Los Possible

Build Up

Paul, McCain, Portman, Pawlenty, Rice, Martinez, Huckabee. One by one they wove a tapestry of ideas, each layer adding more philosophical imagery to the picture, ultimately completed by the Vice Presidential candidate, accepting his party's nomination, Paul Ryan.

Paul, Portman, Pawlenty, and Martinez developed the libertarian themes of individualism, free markets, limited government, balanced budgets, and low taxes. Huckabee touched on these themes, but really seemed to be there to assure the religious right that the Mormon and the Catholic were okay by him.

For four years we have had double digit unemployment for young people, Hispanics, and Blacks ....
- Sen. Rob Portman

In a night rife with self-congratulatory auto-biographical speeches, one politician after another offered anecdotal evidence of friends and family who immigrated to America and built success on their own. Ignoring the irony that they were able to succeed here and not in their nation of origin because of the country we built here, together.

Each governor took a moment, as did Gov Christie the night prior, to point out they had balanced the budget in their state without raising taxes, while having a Democrat legislature. Although none of them mentioned that their state constitutions require that, or the absence of a foreign budget, or the support of federal dollars in their state budgets.

Perhaps the only unexpected theme of the evening was the none to subtle appeal to Asian and Hispanic minorities. Rand Paul used two examples of self made small business immigrants, both SE Asian families cited by name. And several candidates referenced the need for immigration reform, including Gov Martinez citing her own family's realization they were Republican.

I turned to my husband and said, "Well I'll be damned, we're Republican!"
-Gov. Susana Martinez

Gov. Martinez touched on several conservative heart strings as she described her legal immigrant, military veteran, entrepreneurial parents, who started their own security business. Even telling a cute story of how she worked for them guarding a church, with a .375 Smith and Wesson that weighed more than she did, which received a standing ovation.

[We] can not let the Russians and Chinese have a Veto on our foreign policy.
- Sen. John McCain

The American creed of unlimited opportunity.
- Sec. Condoleeza Rice

Sen. McCain and Sec. Rice delivered the Neo Con message to a party which is war and debt weary, but always eager to hear about American exceptionalism and leadership. Reaffirming the doctrines of Monroe, Manifest Destiny, and Cowboy Diplomacy, they declared that unless America provided leadership by taking a strong, military hand in Iran, Afghanistan, and Syria while taking a tougher line with China and Russia, the world would become more dangerous.

Paul Ryan

Eloquent and attractive, Congressman and VP nominee Paul Ryan brought these elements together in a pointed, serious speech long on talking points and short on substance.

Most of the speech was dedicated to describing the current administration as old, weak, tired, desperate, adrift, and lacking leadership. He also made a point to impugn the President's philosophy and skill regarding economics as a central planner who failed to negotiate any trade deals, and instead of creating jobs created debt and a massive new entitlement no one wanted. Leading into his description of Obamacare as massive new entitlement, "which has no place in a free society."

"We can do better!" appears to be the new slogan, as Ryan ticked it off after each critique of the incumbent. Repeatedly promising to provide a better government and economy in grandiose terms, "We are going to solve this nation's economic problems!" However he did not offer any specific programs or cuts to offer us insight as to how this might happen. Throughout the night, we are encouraged to trust Romney because he knows how to be successful, and therefore is best able to make the nation successful

We are going to solve this nation's economic problems
- Rep. Paul Ryan, (R) VP nominee

The few moments in the speech that are not dedicated to attacking the

President, praising Romney, or giving us his own bio, were given to acknowledging the key political themes of the evening. He paused to affirm the Neo Con foreign policy message, the anti-tax/anti-regulation message was well covered, as was the pro-life message, and finally drilling home the idea that the Republicans are the preservers of Medicare.

A Good Night

Overall it was a very good night for the Republicans. Their speakers were articulate and inspiring, and the base will surely be excited after the brutal primary process. They marketed a coherent message that unifies the elements of their party, while providing very few details to be held accountable for later.

Mitt Romney: a leader without followers?

September 19, 2012

A leader without followers is just a man taking a walk.
- unknown

Mitt Romney's inability to gather a following will most likely prove to be the greatest threat to his candidacy.

Aside from the Republican talking heads and party elite who have begun to pillory him in the media, as the scent of danger sends politicians scrambling for cover like the Captain of an Italian cruise ship, the party base has also begun to look elsewhere in organized numbers.

Republicans for Obama, Write in Ron Paul, and the Gary Johnson Libertarian campaign have all begun to draw interest. Individually, no one of these groups would represent a significant challenge to Romney. As a collection, added to the various candidates running in only one state, it could easily add up to 3-5%. If that happens, there is no way for Romney to acquire enough of the swing vote to tip the scales. Even in the best of times, which this is not. Johnson is already polling over 7% in some states.

When you consider that the Republican primary began with a message of "anybody but Obama", and still Romney could not hold their support, even before this last week's fiascos, one's first suspect for failure would be the message.

Reviewing the statements of the three aforementioned groups, it both clarifies and confuses the issue. Those voting for Obama think Romney is too right wing, and want a centrist. The libertarian wing thinks Romney is just like Obama and they want a real conservative. Somehow Romney's plan to offend no one by offering no specifics, backfired into offending everybody.

Ultimately, either internal party politics between the old guard and the TeaParty boxed Romney into an untenable position where he could not campaign on his own ideas, or this guy is the biggest jerk ever. He offers no ideas, presents no passion, and now we find out he holds half of the people in disdain.

As those of us who never planned on voting Republican watch stunned, asking "why is he running?", Republicans are left asking "who am I to vote for?". This is by far the worst tragedy of the Mitt Romney for President campaign; nearly half our electorate was forced by the party elite to accept a candidate they didn't really want, who couldn't get elected and has no business being President if he did. As a result, we all lose out on a vigorous campaign which challenges the incumbent's power and demands a serious discussion of issues. Instead we are forced to watch, helpless, as our choices narrow and the Republic stagnates.

I suspect history will remember this as the election the Republican party died. Born fighting for liberty, its demise ultimately caused by a candidate who did not know his people. What will rise from the ashes is hard to say, but for a period of time the Democrats will be the most powerful party in the most powerful nation with the most powerful military in the world.

Are your better off?
September 5, 2012

The Michelle Obama Doctrine.

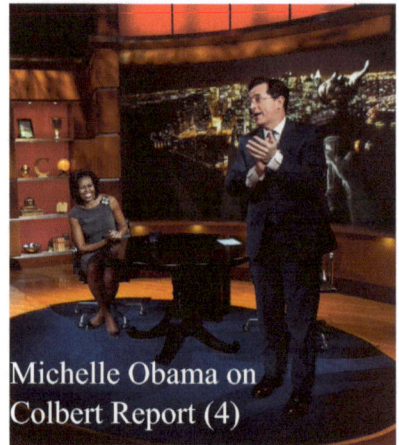

Michelle Obama on Colbert Report (4)

The First Lady headlined the opening night of the Democratic National Convention with a speech universally lauded as a good speech delivered incredibly well by an eloquent and empathic orator. Following earlier speakers' fiery political rhetoric and touching personal stories, Mrs. Obama brought philosophy, personal experience, and practical application together in telling the story of her family's travel from poverty to the White House. Ultimately encapsulating, in this "Michelle Doctrine", the Democrat response to the Republican questions [2], "Are you better off than you were four years ago?" and their accusations about lack of success, in a single sentence about 3/4 of the way through the speech. "Success isn't about how much money you make, it's about the difference you make in people's lives." So this appears to be where the Democrats are trying to set the lynchpin of the argument. While the Republicans, who claim to desire a laissez faire government, yet hold the government responsible for economic success, the Democrats judge the government by the number of people helped.

Success by their Standards?

So let's judge them by their own standards. This graph from MSNBC demonstrates job growth since 2010, a benchmark set by Gov. Romney in a recent CBS interview in which he stated a new President should be allowed six months to a year for his policies to take effec. The graph also displays that overall growth is less than private sector, which is a result of public sector cut backs at all levels. Another way of saying this would be that unemployment was 7.8% when he took office, 9.7% a year later, and 8.3% today.

Is this success by Republican or Democrat definition? Jobs mean more money, and jobs help people, so I suppose you would have to say both. At the same time we have witnessed an increase in welfare recipient numbers from 4.1 Billion in 2009 to 4.6 Billion in 2011. The Republicans would surely not consider this a success, as it deducts from the bottom line without a direct return.

However, for the Democrats this is not only an example of Keynsian, consumer side economics, but also a demonstration of the "Michelle Doctrine". An additional half a billion people surviving the Great Recesssion due to welfare assitance is a significant "difference in people's lives" for better or worse. And if those 4.6 billion Americans had not had welfare, that would be a great deal of inventory left unsold, resulting in a negative impact for the economy and in people's lives.

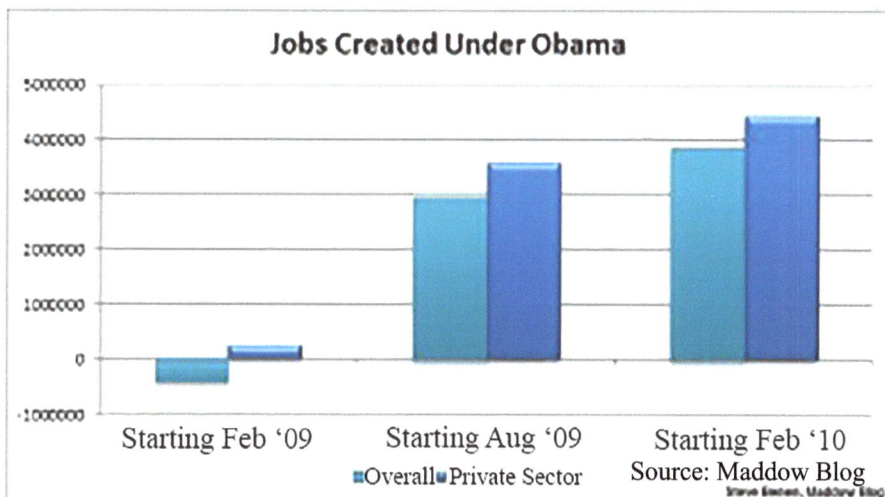

Jobs Created Under Obama

Starting Feb '09   Starting Aug '09   Starting Feb '10
■Overall ■Private Sector   Source: Maddow Blog

The Next Four

So what does this import for our future? Neither party has offered a great deal of detail regarding future plans, but based on limited info we do have, the Wall Street Journal was able to provide a side by side comparison. What we see in the plans provided by the President and his rivals are strategies informed by their stated ideas of success. The Republican plan cuts social expenditures that do not generate returns, while increasing military investments and tax cuts that provide private profits, which they suggest will turn into greater tax revenue as a result of more income existing to tax.

On the other side, we see President Obama offering increases in tax collection, military cuts, and expansions of social services. A budget clearly designed to assist people without concern for corporate profits. Though it must also be noted that the math on the budget seems difficult to balance in either scenario, even less so in the Republican strategy which grows the military and cuts taxes so much greater than it cuts spending. One has to wonder how either party can pay off debt, if they cannot balance an annual budget.

External Links

[2]
http://www.google.com/url?q=http%3A%2F%2Fwww.msnbc.com%2Frachel-maddow-show%2Fthe-misguided-argument-over-net-jobs%3F__utma%3D238145375.1225877798.1344378269.1346288853.1346861611.50%26__utmb%3D238145375.2.10.1346861611%26__utmc%3D238145375%26__utmx%3D-%26__utmz%3D238145375.1346861611.50.21.utmcsr%253Dgoogle%257Cutmccn%253D%2528organic%2529%257Cutmcmd%253Dorganic%257Cutmctr%253Dmsnbc%26__utmv%3D238145375.%257C8%253DEarned%252520By%253Dcable%2

Comparing Budget Plans

Here's how budget proposals or campaign promises from President Barack Obama, former Governor Mitt Romney and Rep. Paul Ryan compare side-by-side.

Proposal	Obama	Romney	Ryan
Individual income taxes	Raise top marginal income tax rate (now 35%) to 39.6%, limit other deductions for upper-income taxpayers. Raise revenue.	Reduce top marginal income tax rate to 28% and reduce other tax rates by 20%. Offset cost by limiting or ending deductions and credit.	Create two new tax brackets, 10% and 25%.
Corporate taxes	Lower top rate (now 35%) to 28%, eliminate tax breaks, provide incentives for manufacturers. Revenue neutral.	Lower top rate to 25%, shift to make it easier for U.S. firms to limit or avoid federal taxes on profits earned overseas. Revenue neutral.	Similar to Romney plan, would lower top rate to 25%, shift to make it easier for U.S. firms to limit or avoid federal taxes on overseas profits.
Medicare	Keep 2010 health law. Change the way the government pays hospitals and other health providers. Raise premiums or copays for some beneficiaries, particularly upper income. Total savings of $248 billion over 10 years.	Repeal the 2010 health-care law. Raise enrollment age to 67 (from 65 today). Offer choice of existing Medicare or new program that would provide vouchers to pay part or all of private-insurance premiums.	Slowly raise eligibility age to 67 and give those younger than 55 the option of a privately run plan paid in part by the government or keeping a Medicare-type plan. No change for those 55 or older. Would cost $205 billion less than White House's budget over 10 years.
Medicaid	Proceed with 2010 law expanding Medicaid, rework the formula on how much federal government gives states the program. Save roughly $72 billion, combined with other changes.	Turn Medicaid into a federal block grant program, giving control and flexibility to states. Unspecified savings.	Turn Medicaid into a federal block grant program, giving control and flexibility to states. Saves $770 billion over 10 years, compared with White House plan, according to Ryan estimate.
Defense spending	About $487 billion in cuts over 10 years from Pentagon's current plan. Appropriate $525 billion for it in fiscal 2013.	Reverse planned Obama cuts, commit at least 4% of GDP toward defense, equivalent to $545 billion in 2013.	Reverse the planned Obama cut, appropriate $554 billion for defense in fiscal 2013.
Deficit	Reduce deficit (now 7.8% of gross domestic product) to 3.9% of GDP by 2014 and 3% of GDP by 2017.	Balance the budget by 2020.	Reduce deficit to 4% of GDP by 2014 and 0.9% of GDP by 2017.

Source: WSJ research

Wall Street Journal

5257Cmsnbc%25257Cmsnbc%252520tv%253D1%255E12%253DLand
ing%252520Content%253DOriginal%253D1%255E13%253DLanding
%252520Hostname%253Dwww.msnbc.msn.com%253D1%255E30%25
3DVisit%252520Type%252520to%252520Content%253DEarned%252
520to%252520Original%253D1%26__utmk%3D269249202&sa=D&sn
tz=1&usg=AFQjCNH_OaJcgK1BydeRMiYqCjPC7AyBDQ

[3]
http://www.google.com/url?q=http%3A%2F%2Fonline.wsj.com%2Fne
ws%2Farticles%2FSB100008723963904440427045775855800439904 5
6%3Fmg%3Dreno64-
wsj%26url%3Dhttp%253A%252F%252Fonline.wsj.com%252Farticle%
252FSB10000872396390444042704577585580043990456.html&sa=D
&sntz=1&usg=AFQjCNEG0xHt6sz4YXHbpG8sDaBe2_awzg

[4]
"Michelle Obama on The Colbert Report" by The White House from
Washington, DC - P041112LJ-0722Uploaded by January. Licensed
under Public domain via Wikimedia Commons -
http://commons.wikimedia.org/wiki/File:Michelle_Obama_on_The_Col
bert_Report.jpg#mediaviewer/File:Michelle_Obama_on_The_Colbert_R
eport.jpg

Clinton speech argues case Obama can't

September 6, 2012

Former President William Jefferson Clinton stepped up to the podium last night and delivered a brilliant, if lengthy, oration praising the work of President Obama and decrying

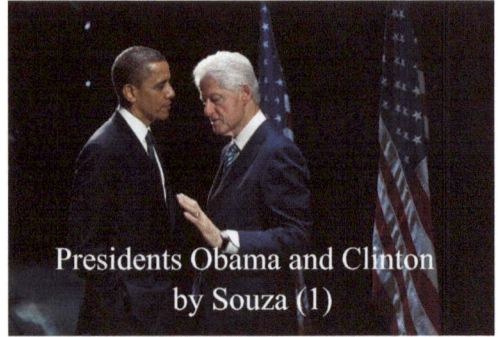

Presidents Obama and Clinton by Souza (1)

the hate and obstructionism of the Republican Congress.

Though the speech was heavy with issues and details, which factcheck.org [2] has confirmed as being factual despite a few exaggerations, he still manages to deliver in a manner that maintains interest and comfort as only Clinton can. His style of homey euphemisms (they're fixing to) combined with the rhetorical method of diverting into colloquial sidebars and then returning to the main point are the way he keeps his audience. Throughout the speech he returns to significant details, admonishing the audience to listen in a grandfatherly way, each point building upon the last, ultimately creating a larger picture.

One of my favorite examples of this last night was the development of the Republicans are bad economists meme. Regardless of whether you agree with Clinton, you have to admire his skill at crafting a speech and delivering oratory.

He opens the speech with a reference to the positive work done by prior Republican Presidents in his lifetime with highways, schools, and welfare. Later, towards the end of the speech, he returns to this theme by applauding the cooperation of past Republicans during his administration and afterwards, while decrying the hate and obstructionism of the current crop. Towards the middle, when offering a defense of Obama's performance, he declares, "No president, no president —not me, not any of my predecessors —no one could have fully repaired all the damage that he found in just four years." A comment carefully crafted to do more than just affirm the good job Obama has done climbing a hard hill. By specifically not mentioning the President after himself, the audience is forced to think of Bush, that Bush caused the damage, that Bush didn't speak at the Republican convention as Clinton is now, which reinforces the idea that they [Republicans] deny the truth. A masterful set up for the next section offering a litany of the President's accomplishments and decrying the attacks against him as an "alternate reality" and "defied arithmetic". In the middle of this, he again sidebars to reflect on the President's ability to work with opposition by listing Republicans and former Democrat opposition who now serve in the cabinet. Reinforcing his own history of working across the aisle, and further isolating the current Republican congress as obstructionist, which gives him the opportunity to again refer to Republican Presidents before and after himself who massively increased the debt. Piece by piece, Bill Clinton built a complex, nuanced message that anyone could understand.

President Obama can not come out tonight and give a speech about why his administration did not go as well as he hoped, or how the Republicans are to blame for anything the voter is unhappy about. For that matter neither can VP Biden. It will just sound like whining. They must deliver inspirational speeches that outline both a vision and a plan for our future. However, they could not just allow the attacks from the Republicans to go unanswered, especially the attacks on leadership, Medicare, and divisiveness. Yet they needed to couch that response in a way that did not seem either defensive or like a little kid screaming, "nu-uh, you are!". This is where President Clinton can deliver like no other.

With a smile, and a grandfatherly wag of the finger, he complements his opponents' predecessors for all the ways they were different. With a mystified expression he (the only modern President to be impeached) questions their partisan attitude. After listing his own, and President Obama's, economic credentials in detail, he points to the absence of detail and poor math results from the Romney/Ryan plans. He comes off polite, reasonable, and rational as he speaks with the voice of experience taking down each and every opposition talking point for the President. Now President Obama is free to talk about moving "forward" without having to address the critiques against him, because they have all been dealt with already.

The only question remaining is can the President, with all his acknowledged skill as a speaker, live up to expectations.

External Links
[1] "Barack Obama and Bill Clinton" by Pete Souza - http://www.flickr.com/photos/whitehouse/7592319076/in/photostream. Licensed under Public domain via Wikimedia Commons - http://commons.wikimedia.org/wiki/File:Barack_Obama_and_Bill_Clint on.jpg#mediaviewer/File:Barack_Obama_and_Bill_Clinton.jpg
[2] http://www.google.com/url?q=http%3A%2F%2Fwww.factcheck.org%2 F2012%2F09%2Four-clinton-nightmare%2F&sa=D&sntz=1&usg=AFQjCNFWnppuR07v9QLBaxW K_ylrxAwlVw

President Obama's Appeal to Community
September 7, 2012

The President's acceptance speech of the Democrat Party's nomination was light on substantive plans for the future, but steeped in a rousing philosophical appeal to the progressive vision he embodies.

As citizens, we understand that America is not about what can be done for us. It's about what can be done by us, together —through the hard and frustrating but necessary work of self-government. That's what we believe.

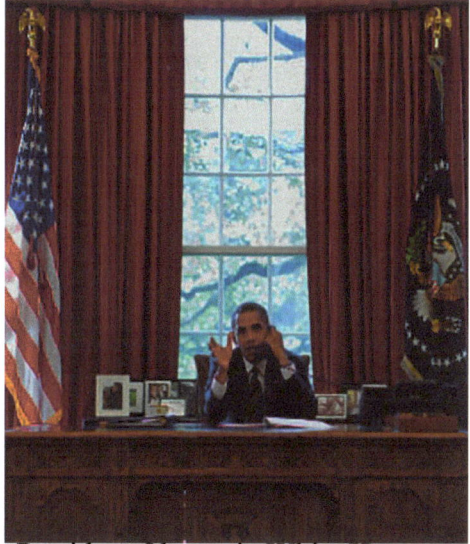

President Obama in White House by Souza (1)

So you see, the election four years ago wasn't about me. It was about you. My fellow citizens —you were the change.
- Pres. Barack Obama

In these two lines he expressed the vision to which the main body of the speech was dedicated. The twin concepts turn the "you didn't build that" critique on its head. By expressing the idea that building together is patriotic duty, he undermines the power of the critique. By expressing the idea his success belongs to everyone who voted for him, he invests the people in his administration and each other. It is the kind of strategy that only a community organizer turned politician could develop.

Unfortunately, the one thing I was most hoping to hear, a detailed plan for the next four years, was absent. He outlined a few principal concepts; Clinton era taxes, fund student loans, green energy investment, job training, and fair immigration policy. But we still don't know how, or what they will look like. Considering that we thought were getting single payer, that's not a minor question.

On the whole, the President accomplished the task before him. He energized the base, he laid out a vision, he stood up for his accomplishments, and he reached out to independents with arguments of math, fairness, and community.

Perhaps the most politically powerful argument may be the unexpected opportunity the Republicans presented on the military and foreign policy. By urging for a future return to NeoCon policies while not mentioning the Afghanistan war at all, they made themselves look callous and aloof. This opens the door for the Democrats to steal a traditionally Republican block in military communities, based on their record of military success and veteran care.

External Links
[1] "President Obama in White House" by Pete Souza - White House (p092812ps-0242) at September 2012: Photo of the Day. Licensed under Public domain via Wikimedia Commons - http://commons.wikimedia.org/wiki/File:President_Obama_in_White_H ouse.jpg#mediaviewer/File:President_Obama_in_White_House.jpg

Keynes v Reagan; the first debate.

September 24, 2012

The first Presidential debate [2], this Oct. 3 in Colorado, will be focused on three topics; economics, the role of government, and governing. Hosted by the near universally respected Jim Lehrer, a former Marine and host of PBS newshour, the ninety minute debate divided into five 15 minute segments promises to be an exposé of applied political and economic philosophy. Unfortunately neither candidate has seemed particularly interested in discussing details of their plans, so we could be hearing a great deal more philosophy than application.

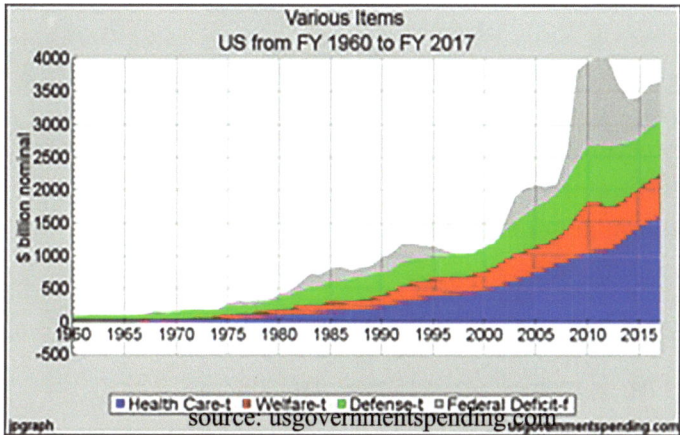

Repeatedly we have been told this is the most important election of our lifetime, because of the choice that we are being presented. However that choice is only defined in the vaguest possible terms. The Republicans define it as between freedom and dependency, while the Democrats set the parameters as community versus greed. The truth is we are being given an option between consumer side, Keynesian economics and supply side, Reaganomics. This is not a new choice, we have been arguing it for 30 years. However, in the wake of the Great Recession, a finer point is placed on the choice this time around. Which ever view wins the election, if the economy turns around, will cement themselves in the minds of the American public as the more valid plan. A forecast made all the more significant by economic predictions [3]of inevitable growth in the next four years regardless.

Heading into this debate, the Republican theory holds the reputation of "got us into this mess", while the Democrat hypothesis bears the slightly less onerous critique "not quite, but getting there". The question will be which candidate can make a better case to a cross section of America. Will President Obama be able to explain that Keynes argues economies are driven by consumers purchasing inventory, thereby forcing the manufacture of more inventory, in persuasive manner? Or will Governor Romney be able to make a more powerful argument on behalf of Reagan that by reducing government participation, the engine of capitalism will run faster, to everyone's benefit? Not exactly stimulating material to work with.

Average Annual Change in Mean Family Income, 1950-2010, by Quintile and for the Top 5 Percent

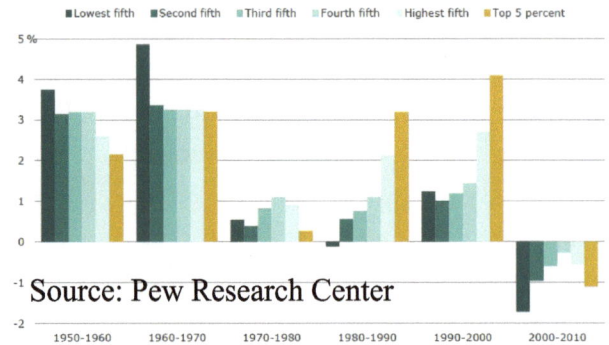

■Lowest fifth   ■Second fifth   ■Third fifth   ▪Fourth fifth   Highest fifth   ■Top 5 percent

Source: Pew Research Center

1950-1960   1960-1970   1970-1980   1980-1990   1990-2000   2000-2010

Source: U.S. Census Bureau, Historical Income Tables, Table F-3 for 1966 to 2010, and derived from Tables F-2 and F-7 for 1950 to 1965. Downloaded from http://www.census.gov/hhes/www/income/data/historical/families/ on July 11, 2012

PEW RESEARCH CENTER

The Keynesian Argument

At it's core, the economic philosophy put forward by John Maynard Keynes, and followed by every President from FDR to Carter, and Clinton, suggests that markets are driven by consumers. The theory being people buy products causing manufacturers to make more inventory to replace it, and that drives growth. In contrast, if large numbers of people are unemployed and unable to make purchases, it sets off a series of dominoes further hurting the economy due to inventory not moving off shelves.

Keynes further argues that the boom/bust cycle which is inherent to a competitive marketplace, also creates instability and opens the door to exploitation. The safety net and entitlements are designed to offset these negatives by keeping currency in the hands of consumers so that when there is a downturn, the unemployed will not serve as the first in a series of negative dominoes due to their inability to buy products. This will, according to the theory, slow both growth and recession by removing (taxing) a portion of the economies profits and using them to fund the safety net. This is also expected to remove the more egregious opportunities for exploitation by removing the dependency on employers for survival.

To the Keynesian, Supply side means choosing more profits while ignoring more human suffering.

The Supply Side Argument

Made famous by Presidents Ronald Reagan and George W Bush, this theory's core argument is that markets are driven by those individuals and businesses who create products and services. Everything that exists in the marketplace is there because these actors put them there, and therefore all market activity flows from them. Under this this theory, growth is stimulated by fertilizing the marketplace for the producers via low taxes, minimal regulations, and government purchases of military technology from the private sector.

To the Supply Side economist the cycles of the marketplace are not a negative that needs to be stabilized. Opportunity lives in these boom/bust cycles, as weak businesses are destroyed during the downturns, room is made in the economy for the growth of new business. New business means new jobs and new technologies and the growth of both the economy and the culture. Artificially supporting consumption doesn't protect workers, it supports failing business, preventing new growth, and thereby keeping people from gaining new employment.

To the Supply Side Economist, Keynesian theory means undermining liberty and the marketplace by making people dependent on government instead of survival of the fittest.

Facts on the Ground

We live in a time when taxes are lower [4]than they have ever been, and the number of recipients of safety net and entitlement funds is higher than ever. At the same time we have an increasing quantity of regulations, and no federal jobs initiative. TARP saved the banks, and the Obama Stimulus package [5] primarily prevented further job loss and offered further middle class tax breaks. We have increased military spending, while only 1% of our population is actively serving in the wars we fight.

These are not examples of plans running concurrently, or in compromise. These are examples of contradictory policies undermining each other. While each side is able to pass some of it's programs but not others, neither theory can effectively execute its plan. The result is an economy stabilizing at the bottom, with millions of consumers requiring assistance and trillions of dollars uninvested by suppliers

As a result,the economy stabilizes at the bottom, with millions of citizens unemployed and receiving assistance, and trillions of dollars sitting in the hands of suppliers not being invested [6].

The Question for the Debates

The question is not which plan would work, either one would work as advertised if allowed to be fully executed. The question is which end result do we desire, a slow growth, stable, government managed economy or a volatile and highly profitable, free market economy? Or do we want the status quo, resulting in a sluggish market encumbered by antithetical governing policies and a public that has no faith in its leadership?

This will be the subject of the first debate. So for the moment the question is, can our candidates deliver an eloquent and insightful discussion? Or will we just get more slogans and backbiting?

External Links

[2]
http://www.google.com/url?q=http%3A%2F%2Fwww.debates.org%2Fi
ndex.php%3Fmact%3DNews%2Ccntnt01%2Cdetail%2C0%26cntnt01ar
ticleid%3D39%26cntnt01origid%3D27%26cntnt01detailtemplate%3Dn
ewspage%26cntnt01returnid%3D80&sa=D&sntz=1&usg=AFQjCNEfY
Q3JJptPJSgX1yRBGslu-RBhPg
[3] http://www.google.com/url?q=http%3A%2F%2Fwww.conference-
board.org%2Fdata%2Fglobaloutlook.cfm&sa=D&sntz=1&usg=AFQjC
NESm3XIfYEN_sxab7UJCBx9fPmeUg
[4]
http://www.google.com/url?q=http%3A%2F%2Ftaxfoundation.org%2Fs
ites%2Ftaxfoundation.org%2Ffiles%2Fdocs%2Ffed_individual_rate_his
tory_nominal%2526adjusted-
20110909.pdf&sa=D&sntz=1&usg=AFQjCNHhGkDOsq3dtJMqZQGrL
X8-sN3tNA
[5]
http://www.google.com/url?q=http%3A%2F%2Fwww.washingtonpost.c
om%2Fblogs%2Fwonkblog%2Fpost%2Fdid-the-stimulus-work-a-
review-of-the-nine-best-studies-on-the-
subject%2F2011%2F08%2F16%2FgIQAThbibJ_blog.html&sa=D&sntz
=1&usg=AFQjCNGnWL_ErxdisPtqQSqGLEibom4Dsg
[6]
http://www.google.com/url?q=http%3A%2F%2Fwww.forbes.com%2Fsi
tes%2Fthesba%2F2011%2F08%2F10%2Fthe-real-reason-for-banks-not-
lending%2F&sa=D&sntz=1&usg=AFQjCNFGqTTfSQO42BmhZushGF
9wduLtBA

Third Party debate, Free and Equal

October 24, 2012

Last night
FreeandEqual.org [2]
hosted a debate among
independent candidates,
moderated by Larry King.
On stage were the Green
Party, Dr. Jill Stein, the
Justice Party, former

Free and Equal Debate (1)

Mayor Rocky Anderson, the Constitution Party, former Congressman
Virgil Goode, and the Libertarian Party, former Governor Gary Johnson.

The debate was short but vibrant, smart, and polite. It was carried on c-
span and Al Jazzera English, but for reasons surpassing understanding,
unless you accept the fiscal conspiracy theories, it received no major
American media coverage. Even accepting the idea that these candidates
have little chance of victory, it is ethically negligent for the fourth estate
to deny information on choices to the American public.

Military Policy and the Security State

This area had universal support on the lectern. For reasons of budget,
constitutional law, and moral imperative, all four candidates agreed that
the United States should immediately end the wars, end drone strikes,
reduce our general military footprint, cut military spending and redirect
spending priorities to the domestic front.

They also all agreed that domestic security programs such as the Patriot
act, the NDAA, etc were not only immoral and unconstitutional, but also
ineffective and should be repealed immediately.

Education

This was the one area of serious disagreement for the evening, federal funding of education. Rocky Anderson and Jill Stein favor increased long term investment. Stein pointing out that the GI Bill had a documented return of 7 dollars of income for every 1 tax dollar spent on education.

Virgil Goode and Gary Johnson both opposed Federal funding for constitutional and budgetary reasons, wanting to leave such efforts to state programs. Gary Johnson suggesting that the federal guarantee was actually driving up tuition costs, and pointing out that when he was Governor they were able to fund higher Ed for citizens in the state without it. Although that last suggests the student loan program didn't exist in NM at the time, which clearly was not so.

Drug War

On this issue there was near total agreement, Virgil Goode being the hold out. The other three candidates all agreed that the drug war is a failed policy which needed to end. They viewed addiction as a medical issue which needed to be treated as such. Dr. Stein pointing out that if science were used to classify drugs marijuana would not be a scheduled illegal drug. Industrial hemp also figuring into this discussion as evidence of the foolishness of the drug war, preventing a non drug cash crop from being used simply because it is similar to a classified drug.

Summary

A well run and interesting debate with specific plans on important issues. These candidates know they are not going to win, but they are passionate about their cause and their ideas, and they put forward logical sounding plans. None of that is bad for our nation. So why, why, will our major media not give them the time of day necessary for them to build the type of support required to be considered legitimate in the first place?

External Links
[1] By Connie Ma (Flickr: Rocky speaks.) [CC-BY-SA-2.0 (http://creativecommons.org/licenses/by-sa/2.0)], via Wikimedia Commons
[2] https://www.google.com/url?q=https%3A%2F%2Fwww.freeandequal.or g%2F&sa=D&sntz=1&usg=AFQjCNE_F2aS9w_zX-UsjmHBoe7bnvR_ww

On Election Night, Stein Rubs Johnson the Wrong Way

Nov. 5, 2012

In Washington, DC tonight there was a debate between Green Party Candidate Dr. Jill Stein and Libertarian Candidate Gov. Gary Johnson. Organized and hosted by Free and Equal, an organization dedicated to gaining recognition for third party candidates. It was, perhaps, one of the most passionate and honest debates no one will ever see.

Both candidates agreed that we needed to end the drug war, the foreign wars for oil, the Patriot Act, the use of drones at home and abroad, blamed the Republicans and Democrats alike for these problems, and both accused President Obama of committing grievous civil rights violations and running a police state.

On Foreign Aid they both agreed it was marred by unintended consequences. Johnson connected our aid to Pakistan, defended by the administration as necessary because they have nukes, to rogue nations like Iran pursuing nukes. Stein pointed to foreign aid as military aid and connected it to terrorist groups getting weapons on the black market. On Iran, she argued for a nuclear free planet, weapons and energy, beginning with the middle east, though she did not say how that would be accomplished.

They also both agreed that current economic polices cause many of our problems, though on solutions to these problems significant philosophical differences were unveiled.

Dr. Stein, over the course of the evening, argued in support of various aspects of the "Green New Deal". It is the central point of her campaign, that the Green Party appears to be hanging its future arguments on. They state that this plan can create full employment while resolving our environment crisis, and dealing with the banks and the foreign policy problems, all at once. By cutting our military footprint abroad, and reallocating that money to debt and green projects, including converting the military-industrial complex, increasing taxes, and ending drug war costs while taxing profits, we can build the nation into prosperity. Citing FDR's policies as proof of the value of government investment. She also intends to end all student debt and make college education free, citing the GI bill as proof of education investment value.

Gov. Johnson was a strong advocate for laissez faire economic policies, including a zero corporate and income tax rate, instead favoring the Fair Tax which is a national sales tax with a rebate. He argued for no foreign aid, no regulations, FEMA as a coordinator of state and private resources only. He also argued that gouging would be better than government price fixing limiting sales opportunities in disaster zones, citing the gas lines in post Sandy areas as an example of the negative impact of regulations.

Whenever Dr. Stein argued in favor of some social policy, Gov. Johnson would become extremely upset, gesticulating widely and vehemently arguing that austerity was the only way out of our economic problems. Dr. Stein would retort in a calm, professorial tone with historical examples of her theory working, and mock austerity and laissez faire theory "…if there's ever been an example of it working, I wish someone would tell me." Johnson pounded away at the theme, suggesting through intonation that it should be common sense, "if you tax something there's less of it." Although he did not answer her historical question, or explain why public investment was not valuable in the absence of private investment.

Neither of these candidates believes they are going to win tomorrow. They are both, clearly, laying the groundwork for long term party plans. Which suggests they see opportunity in the near future. An opportunity that only arises if one of the two current parties begins to crumble. Historically, in the United States, third parties have arisen to prominence as another party died off; the Whigs and the Republicans being two major examples. The only possible way for that to transpire this election is if the Republicans lose.

The Republicans are facing a demographic base that is shrinking to such an extent, that after this election they will have to change their approach or risk an ever diminishing share of the political power pie. They also face a Tea Party who was forced to accept Romney on the promise he was the only candidate who could win because he was moderate. So they will be angry, and stepping further away from them, towards Hispanics for example, could cause them to revolt and leave the party. The could end up joining the Libertarians or forming their own party. Either way, the Democrats will be the only major party remaing, which will open the door for a new party on left and right, because Americans love an underog and hate monopolies.

An International View of Election 2012
October 10, 2012

While waiting for President Obama to arrive for his rally at OSU yesterday, I began interviewing members of the audience. For the most part I encountered exactly what you would expect, young students who had already decided to vote for Obama this year. I did meet a handful of undecideds, and one young African American who intended to vote for Gary Johnson, the Libertarian candidate, because he considered himself a pacifist. However, the most interesting conversation I had was with two foreign born attendees.

One man, a 31 year old Iranian lawyer with American citizenship who had immigrated three years ago, refused to give his name because he still wished to visit his homeland and feared that government's actions should it discover his words, so I will simply call him Ahmed. He knows well what the Iranians are capable of, as he served on the defense team for Roxana Saberi, a Japanese journalist falsely jailed for 8 years as a spy. Now Ahmed is attending law school all over again, in America, so that he can work in his profession here.

Ahmed told me he was there because he supported the President, intended to vote for him, and was extremely excited to see him "face to face". When I asked why he preferred Obama to Romney, it was primarily a foreign policy response.

He saw the idea of accelerating the war footing a waste of money, as it would cause further spread of Al Queda. He considers Ahmadinejad to be head of the Iranian government, but not the people. Despite this, the talk of war seemed foolish to him, as these wars rarely accomplish anything beyond destruction.

Perhaps Ahmed's most passionate criticism was for those Americans who complain about loss of liberty, *"I just want to tell them to shut up... They don't know what it is to lose freedom."*

Standing next to Ahmed was a German citizen visiting family in America, Daniel Lenhert age 30. A professor of criminology, Daniel and his associates in Germany are generally supportive of President Obama and hopeful he will win this election. They see his economic policy as being more stable and humane, and his foreign policy as being more wise.

On the middle east, they are pleased to see a President provide some limits to Israel regarding Palestinian policy. On Iran, they approve of his policy to pursue diplomatic pressure before rushing into war.

While the young Germans don't approve of the imperialistic use of NATO, they don't want to see our bases leave as they provide significant economic benefits. Overall there is a positive view of the US military in a nation that still views us as their saviors from both fascism and communism.

Daniel viewed our media as a "propaganda" machine and described the political campaigns as "the show". Of course he did not suggest things were any different in his homeland, just more extreme here.

When I asked these men what people in the world thought when they heard American politicians refer to the US as the greatest nation in the world, they just smiled and shrugged, "it's just part of the show".

I found it fascinating how focused the rest of the world is on our political cycles, while most Americans are probably unaware of whom Merkel and Ahmadinejad are, or what titles they hold. Friends who were in Korea in 2008, tell stories of a nation celebrating over our election of Obama. I don't think most of us are aware of the full impact that our government, and therefore our votes, have on the nations and people of the world.

2 dull in Ohio

Akron, Ohio, 9/26/12

Mother Nature commented on the campaign today, providing a grey, soggy, morose backdrop for the candidates' dueling speeches in Northern Ohio. A fitting commentary for rhetorical blandness absent inspiration or programs.

In three separate speeches, accompanied by minor celebrities unrelated to national politics, Mitt Romney informed [2] his audience that we have a massive debt, high unemployment, education challenges, and a trade imbalance with China. For solutions he offered his election, tax cuts, good teachers, and tough talk. Repeatedly he blamed the President for not doing these things, unfortunately, the record shows the President has actually done all of these things (except elect Romney of course). In perhaps the most bizarre twist of the day, Romney reminded his audience on several occasions that he does care and then used Romneycare as proof.

I think throughout this campaign as well, we talked about my record in Massachusetts, don't forget —I got everybody in my state insured,
- Gov. Mitt Romney, Republican Candidate for President

President Obama gave two speeches [3] before the communities of Bowling Green and Kent State Universities. As expected, the majority of the speech is dedicated to mocking his opponent's ideas as out of touch, cold, and mathematically incoherent. For his own part he, of course, trumpeted his own accomplishments over the last four years regarding health care, China, and stimulus. Moving forward he recommended the now standard concepts of Clinton era tax rates and 100,000 new jobs. However, halfway through the speech in Bowling Green he dropped in two sentences which proffered a concept I have never heard him suggest before. The President put forward the idea of taking the subsidies away from oil and re- allocating them to alternative fuels. Not a new idea, but a first for a sitting President.

Let's take that money we're giving to companies that are already hugely

profitable —every time you go to the pump, they're making money; they don't need a tax break. Let's use that money and invest in wind and solar and clean coal technology. (Applause)
- President Barack Obama, Democrat incumbent

Ohio is purported to be one of the most important battle ground states because no Republican has ever won the Presidency without it. Yet the battle appears to consist of little more than showing up for speeches and paying for commercials. Content consists mostly of self praise and opponent mocking, with the occasionally vague promise. In an election billed as the most important of our lifetime, our candidates seem to have a peculiar lack of big ideas or specific plans.

External Links
[1]
http://www.google.com/url?q=http%3A%2F%2Fjdadler.com%2F2dullin ohio%2F&sa=D&sntz=1&usg=AFQjCNFU8989Kaaic8ZtvcMhRwYpZ KErwA
[2] https://www.youtube.com/watch?v=xVGlEh5TfC4
[3]
http://www.google.com/url?q=http%3A%2F%2Fwww.whitehouse.gov% 2Fthe-press-office%2F2012%2F09%2F26%2Fremarks-president-campaign-event-bowling-green-oh&sa=D&sntz=1&usg=AFQjCNEq8NLobUpTz5cbSreO4tdPlQ9tCQ

Will Conservatives turn to Gary Johnson?
September 19, 2012

Observing the spectacular debacle that is the Mitt Romney for President campaign, one can not help but think, How can he run a country if he can't run a campaign? Based on the critiques being put forward by Republican talking heads, they are starting to wonder that too. Joe Scarborough ventured the hypothetical that if Romney failed at the first debate, and you saw Rove et al starting to focus on Congressional races, that would mean the party had given up on him.

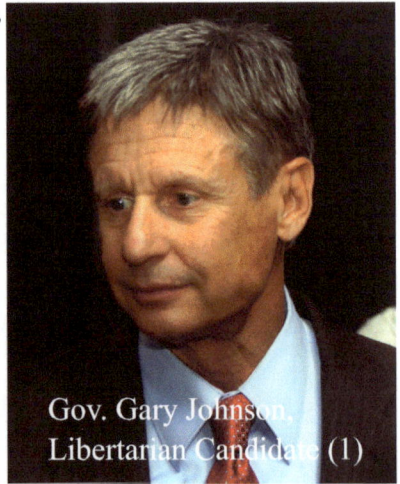

Gov. Gary Johnson, Libertarian Candidate (1)

This sent the wheels in my cranium spinning into potential alternate scenarios, the most practical of which involved the TeaParty/Paulites deciding to abandon the party and take up the Libertarian banner. The Libertarian candidate, Gary Johnson, is on the ballot in all fifty states, so viable theoretically. He is a former Republican Governor of New Mexico, noted for successfully applying conservative budget values in a Democrat state. On the issues he holds an odd mix of values that, individually, appeal to many groups, but as a group may not appeal to any.

Fiscally he is conservative; cut spending and taxes. But the details become more difficult to align with all sides as he wants to close all overseas military presence, end the drug war, and close departments like housing and energy.

Civil Rights is a fairly liberal position, though based on conservative philosophy of limited government. He is pro-choice, except late term. He supports gay marriage. Generally he stands for equality under the law.

On immigration he holds the same position as every president for 30 years; work visas and secure the border.

Education and Health Care he believes should be left to the states and competition, with the fed only providing support via block grants. And for the Internet he believes in "net neutrality" and deregulation.

While current Republicans might have trouble with certain elements of his policies, the majority of his views match trends in public views. More importantly, it is clear exactly what he believes, and he can deliver the message in a coherent, confident manner.

I don't really expect the Republic base to turn to the Libertarians en masse this year, however the question remains, what are the Republican electorate to do when the party-chosen candidate does not represent them?

External Links
[1] "Gary Johnson by Gage Skidmore 3" by Gage Skidmore - Flickr: Gary Johnson. Licensed under Creative Commons Attribution-Share Alike 2.0 via Wikimedia Commons - http://commons.wikimedia.org/wiki/File:Gary_Johnson_by_Gage_Skid more_3.jpg#mediaviewer/File:Gary_Johnson_by_Gage_Skidmore_3.jpg
[2] http://www.google.com/url?q=http%3A%2F%2Fwww.garyjohnson2012 .com%2F&sa=D&sntz=1&usg=AFQjCNFPeQvf4JR1_CMyQKvtlile0N 4vaQ

Cheri Honkala, Green Party Candidate for VP

October 19, 2012

Recently, I had the opportunity to interview Cheri Honkala [2], Green Party Vice Presidential candidate. In a cozy waiting room outside a radio studio where she had just done an on-air interview. We sat and talked for a few minutes before she rushed off to her next event. Exhausted from a non stop schedule in which Ms. Honkala and Presidential Candidate Dr. Jill Stein have championed environmental protection and workers rights, only to be ignored by the press at every turn and repeatedly arrested for daring to voice their their opinions in public, as they were the other day outside the Hofstra debates. [3]

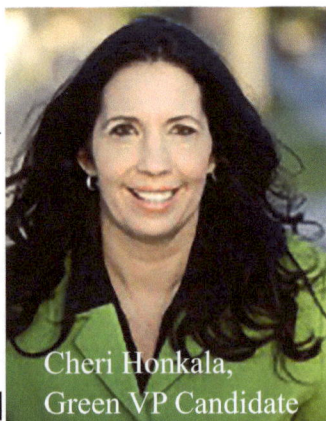

Cheri Honkala, Green VP Candidate

Any discussion with the Green Party candidates has to focus on the bold concept of full employment outlined in the Green New Deal. [4] I began by questioning the practicality of the concept, not only financially but also in the implementation of actually finding positions for everyone. Honkala did not hesitate to respond positively. Outlining a fiscal plan that would be redirecting resources from a reduced military footprint abroad, and altering our welfare system to one where people who receive benefits are contributing, along with a tax plan that not only increases the progressive scale on the top bracket but also adds a tax on executive bonuses, that when combined will provide the necessary funding. As to the actual work being done, Honkala describes a modern WPA that includes the arts, infrastructure projects, sustainable farms, urban community farming, investments in green energy projects, and redevelopment of the over 6000 abandoned and collapsing homes in America.

I questioned the viability of this on two fronts, a) how would we get everyone, even the lazy, to actually work and 2) was this a sustainable long term plan after the initial projects had been completed? Honkala dismissed both ideas as myths. Even the so called 'welfare queen' has to earn in some manner, even if it's under the table now, because the limited funds currently supplied through welfare don't provide enough to sustain a family. According to her, and she is someone who has worked her way out of homelessness, all our current system does is drive people into the black market. She also perceived scarcity as a construct of global capitalism which has "misplaced priorities" on profits and military expansion rather than education and agriculture networks.

Pointing to NAFTA and the TPP as examples of this, Honkala described these international treaties as effectively providing cheap labor for international corporations and cheap goods for Americans while undermining labor, the middle class, and environmental concerns. Giving a nod to Ross Perot, she pointed out this was all predicted and has continued unabated.

Practical?

While its difficult to tabulate the exact numbers, it is hard to argue with the logic that by reallocating military spending and collecting a few more tax dollars, and redirecting our welfare programs all into a modern WPA, we could employ vast numbers of our unemployed population. The chief obstacle appears not to be fiscal or application, but rather how to motivate America to accept such a dramatic shift in philosophy. The Green Party's "Green New Deal" appears to be a practical step towards better branding and messaging, however they still need to overcome the hurdle of near total media blackout of their voice.

External Links

[1]
http://www.google.com/url?q=http%3A%2F%2Fjdadler.com%2Fcheri-
honkala-green-candidate-for-
vp%2F&sa=D&sntz=1&usg=AFQjCNEqQd5phDmR04Di9Hm2AkxJtE
Llmg
[2]
http://www.google.com/url?q=http%3A%2F%2Fwww.jillstein.org%2Fc
heri_honkala&sa=D&sntz=1&usg=AFQjCNHJ1B3oeLHWIHD6USzv
O2RDCkBeLA
[3]
http://www.google.com/url?q=http%3A%2F%2Fwww.jillstein.org%2F
mockumentary_debate&sa=D&sntz=1&usg=AFQjCNG1uSiIaYwCe-
MAuHrFIMiwICkkBw
[4]
http://www.google.com/url?q=http%3A%2F%2Fwww.jillstein.org%2Fg
reen_new_deal&sa=D&sntz=1&usg=AFQjCNFyLDarVdH3sIeRxygBV
UnsFg0g5w

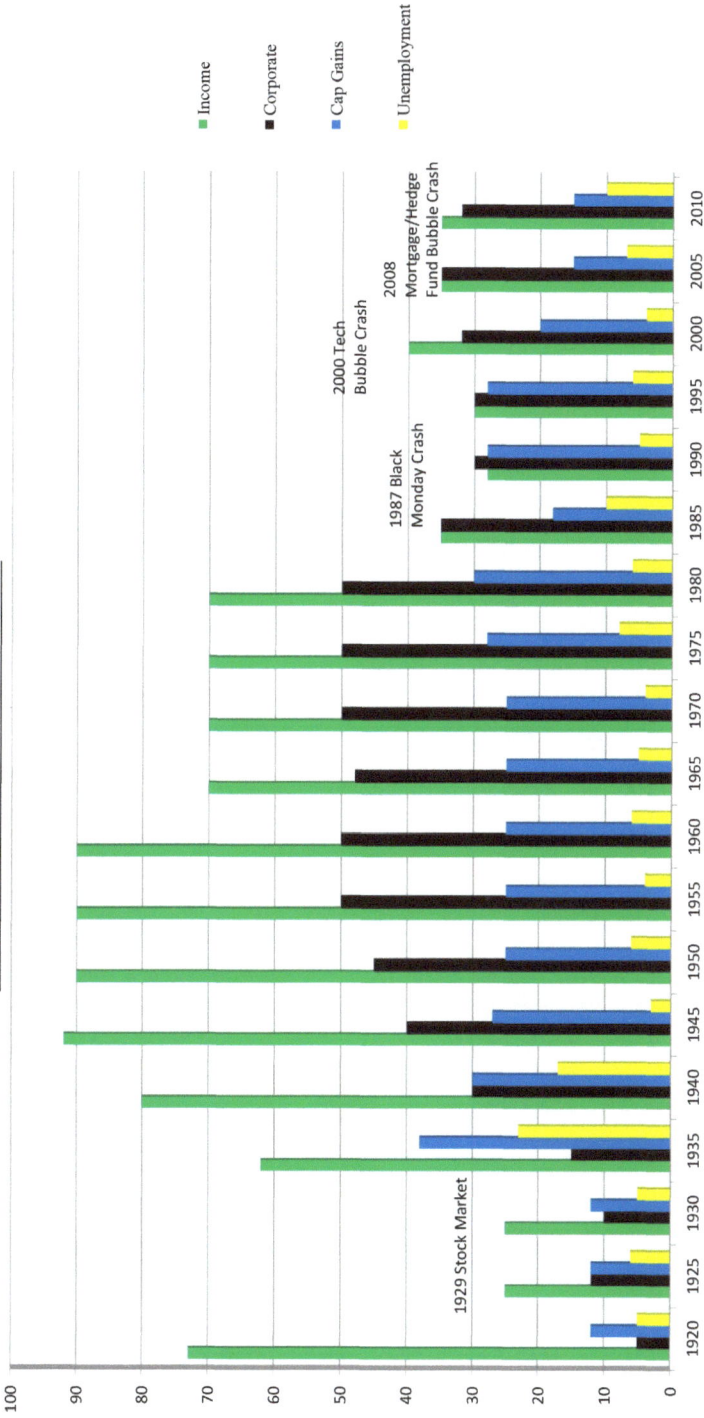

US Federal Maximum Tax Rates and

Source: Treasury, OMB,

Legend:
- Income (green)
- Corporate (black)
- Cap Gains (blue)
- Unemployment (yellow)

Annotations:
- 1929 Stock Market
- 1987 Black Monday Crash
- 2000 Tech Bubble Crash
- 2008 Mortgage/Hedge Fund Bubble Crash

Columbus, Ohio
October 2012

Columbus 2012 is a city on the verge. It's on the verge of becoming a boom town or sinking into despair. There are cute neighborhoods with coffee shops, bars, delis, and shopping where middle class people can walk and enjoy an afternoon. There are also neighborhoods, just a few blocks over, with empty houses and check cashing places next to dollar stores. Public transit exists, but the bus drove by me, while standing at the stop, on three separate occasions. Apparently, this is a recurring problem in Columbus.

Walking the hour and half from the Greyhound station toward the house I would be staying at, I encountered the best bookstore I have ever visited, The Book Loft. Set in a Civil War era building, it has 32 rooms that require navigating narrow aisles and winding stairwells to visit. If you figure out the map, you could search by topic, but it's much more fun to simply wander aimlessly and discover what is behind each corner. I could easily have spent my entire trip walking the old wooden shelves, finding some hidden nook to sit in and paging through a collection of dusty books.

same street, Columbus, Ohio, 2012

A few blocks further, the trees become sparse, the buildings begin to show signs of age, bank-sale signs pop up, and as I approach the intersection before their home, gas station, liquor store, and pizza delivery places populate the landscape. Following my iphone gps, I cut down a side street, alternately decorated with cute fenced in yards and busted cars, finding my destination mid block. I am reminded of the season by the dramatically carved pumpkins throughout the neighborhood.

A covered porch leads to a door, set back on the right. My knock is answered by a young brunette in large framed glasses. She questions my identity vigorously before allowing me entry. I soon discover she is not one of the residents, but rather the tutor for the home-schooled autistic child that lives there, which was news to me. He was obviously on the

Left to Right: Dean Popiel, Yoshi, Tara Mullins-Cosme, Joel Cosme

better end of the spectrum, as he was able to interact with me like a normal kid the entire time I was there. Apparently, the limited stimulus of a home with only a few adults was controllable, while the wide world with constant changing stimuli would set off chaotic behavior. The kid I got know was all smiles and curiosity with a mischievous sense of humor.

I would meet the parents a few hours later, but first I would meet their roommate, Dean Popiel. Towering over people at 6'4"-6'5", a veteran of US engagement in Beirut, Lebanon during the 80s, Dean had to trudge the long road through PTSD before such a label existed or soldiers were allowed to acknowledge war left scars on their mind. Now he dedicated his life to developing anonymous support for any and all veterans who simply needed to talk without fear of personal embarrassment.

The homeowners and parents, Tara Mullins and Joel Cosme, came home separately over the next few hours. Between their two incomes, along with rent from their tenant Dean, they pulled together enough for their normal overhead plus the expenses of a special needs child. Yet they maintained a beautiful 2 story home, with nice back yard, a generally happy environment, and the generosity to offer strangers like myself a free place to stay.

I wanted to repay them in some way, so I offered to make dinner. Tara suggested we go to her grandfather's place, because he was a character and I would enjoy meeting him. She wasn't lying. As we drove out, the skies opened up and rain so thick you could not see beyond the windshield dumped onto central Ohio. Adding to the adventure, people began pulling over to the side to wait it out, but you would have no way of knowing this, or how far they actually pulled over, until practically on top of them.

By the time we arrived, the storm had let up. The veil lifted, and I found myself in the middle of a great, empty expanse of farmland. No signs of civilization in any direction. I began to wonder if these sweet, generous people were about to drag me into a dark basement and sacrifice me to Satan, when the headlights illuminated a mailbox and Joel announced we had arrived.

Turning up the winding driveway, a tilted box of a house appeared at the far end. Karen told me her grandfather built the house himself. I believed her. Roughly the size of a two bedroom apartment, I'm not sure any of the corners were square. But this structure had stood, with repairs, since the depression era. Suggesting it has more structural integrity than most mcmansions.

The door opened on an elf-like man, maybe 5'5", balding, crooked nose, back bent with age and deaf as a tree stump. He welcomed me warmly, and began giving a tour of his home, describing how he had made each and every one of his possessions, except the fridge and stove which were fairly new additions apparently; cutlery, tables, chairs, pots and pans, all made by his hands. At 97, he still chopped his own wood for heat, cleaned his pistol and walked the property daily inspecting animal traps. Meeting this man, I felt like a complete wimp and was sure that my entire generation would die if the power supply were cut for more than a week.

I stayed in Columbus for almost two weeks. I gathered several significant interviews, saw the President speak at Ohio State University, and met a handful of interesting citizens. Perhaps the most interesting part of my time here, were the 3rd party interviews I garnered; two Libertarian house candidates, a Green house candidate and the Green VP candidate, Cheri Honkala. The thing about 3rd party candidates is that they already know they aren't going to win, so they are in it for the message rather than attaining power for themselves. These are the kind of candidates you wish were in the debates, because they are so passionate about everything they say. Though one has to wonder, if they did gain prominence, would they be as easily corrupted as all those who have come before.

If you ever want to truly understand how money affects our politics, compare the 3rd party debates to the major party debates. The major parties will appear more polished and the answers more practiced and vague, because they hire people to teach them this. The 3rd party candidates will have more data, offer detailed plans, and be far more passionate, but their public speaking skills will be of a lesser quality. Yet you will have never heard more than rumors about these 3rd party candidates because popular media only covers candidates who are already polling well, which requires advertising dollars. And so, a functional duopoly continues.

President Obama rally, OSU

Via Twitter, September-November 2012

New Earth @2newearth
World Does Not Have Forever: either Pres Obama leads on climate change, civil liberties, ending perma-war, or little different from Romney

SuperSam @cantaxpro
#taxsupport.ca Reader's view: What is Romney hiding by not releasing tax returns?: He can dispel these shadows o... bit.ly/QNuJO6

Jonathan S @jonathansholar
@joerogan #rapeculture meets #murderculture Todd Akin gets Karl Rove apology for murder joke newyork.newsday.com/news/nation/to...

AP Politics @ap_politics
Obama duels Romney and Ryan over coping with college costs as parties compete for young voters:apne.ws/RwtUnL #Election2012

Huffington Post @huffingtonpost
Bill Maher on Obama's debate performance: 'looks like he took my million and spent it all on weed' huff.to/RI0M0N

AlterNet @alternet
Jon Stewart on Fox Coverage of Romney "47%" Video: "Chaos on Bullsh*t Mountain" alternet.org/hot-news-views...

LibertyPoet @libertypoet
@LibertyPoet @dailypaul "The 2012 debates brought to you by Goldman Sachs" or "Mitt Romney & Barack Obama" :)

Red Alert Politics @redalert
Ryan: Gun Owners Should Fear an Obama Re-Election bit.ly/SY04JI via @nationaljournal

Jest Aries @kryl_niterane
Rich people claiming to be victimized after Obama bailed them out AND let them continue their business practices. Fuck you rich bitches

Down Ticket Races

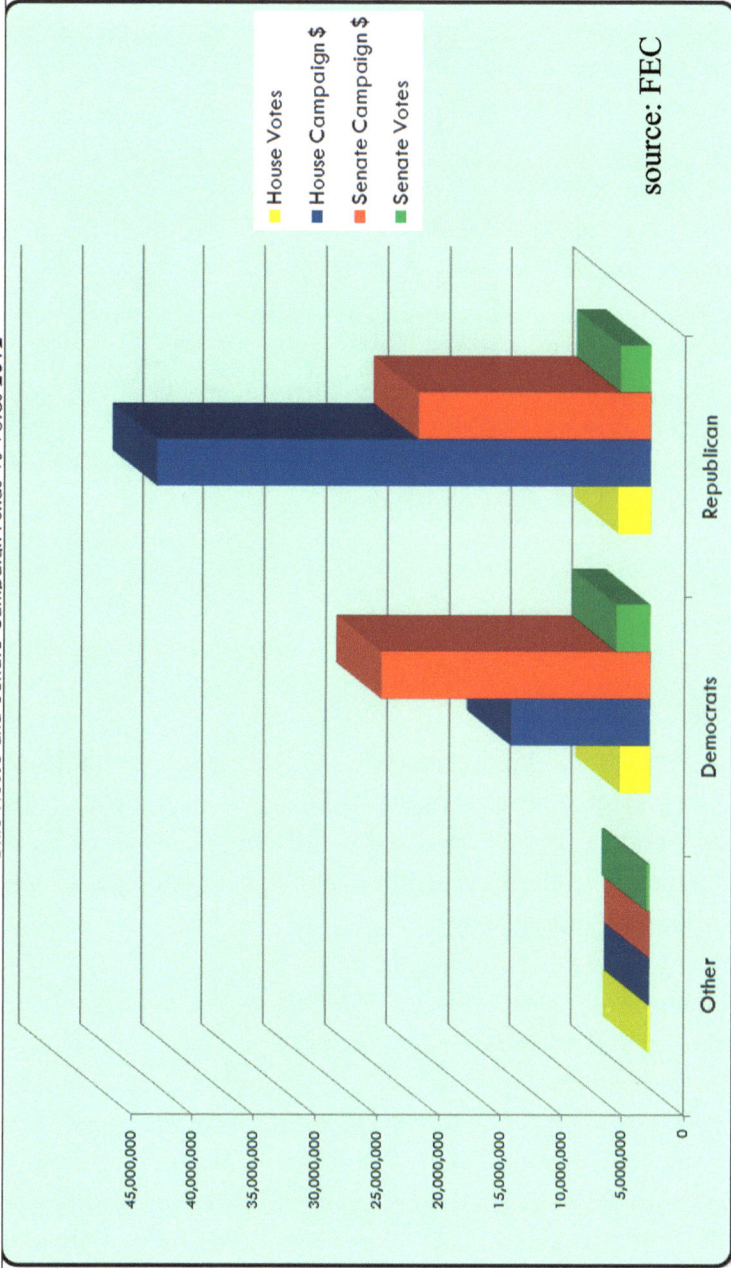

Ohio House and Senate Campaign Funds Vs Votes 2012

Legend:
- House Votes
- House Campaign $
- Senate Campaign $
- Senate Votes

source: FEC

State Supreme Court, Ohio 10/04/12

On a brisk, sunny, autumn day in Dayton, Ohio a group of Democrats gathered at Flannigans Pub to support State Senator Skindell's campaign for the Ohio Supreme court. Surrounded by Irish mythological

symbology and local, working class color, Commissioners, Judges, and assorted campaign officials huddled about the four foot high plastic table top to strategize for the final push to November 6. During a break in their session, I had the opportunity to interview Sen. Skindell.

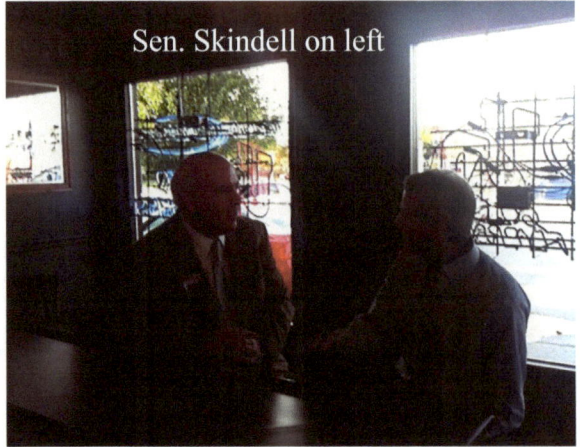

Sen. Skindell on left

Senator Mike Skindell, Ohio

One thing is for sure, Skindell has not lost any passion in his 14 plus years holding elected office. Emphatically arguing for the need to add balance to a court currently occupied by 6 Republicans and 1 Democrat, he decried the group-think created by having a common philosophy on such an important judicial body.

"Determining legal doctrine requires debate among multiple viewpoints... It's about balance and fairness."

Skindell certainly offers a differing viewpoint from his opponent on the ballot, Incumbent Judge O'Donnell. Whereas O'Donnell's rulings tend to fall in line with the traditional conservative view of law and business, Skindell's legislative record has favored the more liberal roots of the Democrat part in Ohio. Supporting a moratorium on death penalties until a current study is completed, favoring public funding of campaigns, fought to lift medical gag orders related to fracing, and recently fighting the financing of Jobs Ohio.

Jobs Ohio

Although this was a legislative issue for him, which he admitted would require his recusal if it came before a court he sat on, the Constitutional argument he makes offers some insight to voters. Jobs Ohio [1] is a public/private partnership *"designed to lead Ohio's job-creation efforts by singularly focusing on attracting and retaining jobs, with an emphasis on strategic industry sectors."* While Skindell says he has no objection to the principal, the organization of it does trouble him, legally. There are number of aspects [2] that he sees as problematic, but the fundamental Constitutional problem the Senator points to is its financing. He argues that the state has used public equity and good faith to support the private non-profit and that violates provisions created by the people during the Constitutional Convention of 1850.

As it turns out, after reading through the lengthy and dense document, Article VIII Section 4 [3] does appear to prohibit public/private partnerships.
Credit of State; the State Shall Not Become Joint Owner or Stockholder
The credit of the state shall not, in any manner, be given or loaned to, or in aid of, any individual association or corporation whatever; nor shall the state ever hereafter become a joint owner, or stockholder, in any company or association in this state, or elsewhere, formed for any purpose whatever.

If the plaintiffs in the case currently working its way through the Ohio courts are able to demonstrate that the funding for Jobs Ohio violates this article, then it seems difficult to envision how the courts could rule against the Senator's allies on this. Which would vindicate Skindell's interpretation of the Constitution against that of the Govenor and other Republicans.

Balance

When asked why voters should unseat O'Donnell in particular, a Judge with 30 years experience, the Senator made his most empassioned case for balance. Pointing out that O'Donnell has been reputed not only as a favored judge by the Chamber of Commerce, but also reported to vote with his donors 91% of the time [4].

He [O'Donnell] is extreme. The NY Times said he is out of balance, voting with contributors 91% of the time.

(author's note: In fairness, neither of these facts prove anything, but as circumstantial evidence they would be considered highly prejudicial)

On the issue of experience Skindell seemed unconcerned, pointing out that, in addition to his 14 years making law, he had 10 years as an administrative judge for the department of health, which is more than the 40 US Supreme Court judges who had never worked as a judge prior to their appointments.

External Links
[2]
http://www.google.com/url?q=http%3A%2F%2Fwww.hudsonhubtimes.com%2Fnews%2Farticle%2F5206521&sa=D&sntz=1&usg=AFQjCNHNzrKNjb0hVOVU21ZYR7WANUM7ag
[3]
http://www.google.com/url?q=http%3A%2F%2Fwww.ballotpedia.org%2Fwiki%2Findex.php%2FArticle_VIII%2C_Ohio_Constitution&sa=D&sntz=1&usg=AFQjCNFBdNOq-DaLmrbr1azfX5ahMUsmSw
[4]
http://www.google.com/url?q=http%3A%2F%2Fjonathanturley.org%2F2008%2F03%2F23%2Fohio-supreme-court-criticized-for-ruling-overwhelmingly-in-favor-of-campaign-donors%2F&sa=D&sntz=1&usg=AFQjCNGdnaH7bMxs7bYaEB8CiFUei1gRcw

Via Twitter Septmber - November 2012

Malachi @chrstcap
Complete results of Ohio Election 2012
www2.sos.state.oh.us/pls/enrpublic/... (look at US Congress, see RINO
Speaker John Boehner got 99.86% of the vote)

Kelly @klsouth
#Ohio Demands the Truth on Benghazi (Ohio Tea Party rally Sunday,
Nov 4, 2012, Cincinnati) bit.ly/RyTMUC #Cincy #tcot #Bearcats

Ronald Jackson @ronaldjackson
The Repubicans Plan To STEAL the 2012 Elections: "How The Tea
Party Hopes To Purge Thousands of Ohio Voters" tiny.cc/1andlw

Yahoo @yahoo
Naked protesters storm Boehner's office yhoo.it/SoQNhW Three women
are arrested in the House speaker's suite next to the Capitol.

Huffington Post @huffingtonpost
Boehner: GOP won't agree to raise taxes on wealthy, even if Obama wins
huff.to/RJADLF

Huffington Post @huffingtonpost
Harry Reid on John Boehner: "I don't understand his brain"
huff.to/ShLNu8

JORGE RAMOS @jorgeramosnews
What a change!!! Speaker Boehner: "I think a comprehensive approach
is long overdue..we can find common ground (on immigration)".

Ezra Klein @ezraklein
Boehner's "mandate" is complicated by the fact that House R's won by
redistricting, not by getting more votes: washingtonpost.com/blogs/ezra-
kle...

US House races in Ohio
9/18/2012

Ohioans are facing, not only a heavily contested Presidential race for their state, but also races for the US House of Representatives that are dramatically different than prior years.

Changes in population resulted in redistributing that cost Ohio two seats in the House, now having 16 instead of 18. This also meant that the remaining districts had to be redrawn to properly serve the public and meet the Constitutional requirements. As a result, several Representatives found themselves either without districts or in new districts.

Tim Ryan(D) incumbent from the newly defunct 17th is now running in the 13th district against (R)Marisha Agana. The incumbent from the former 13th district borders, Betty Sutton(D), is now running in the 16th district against incumbent Jim Renacci(R), a rare occasion where two incumbents compete. And Bob Gibbs(R) incumbent from the 18th district is now running in the 7th district against Joyce Healy-Abrams(D). While Dennis Kuccinch(D) from the 10th has decided that without his original constituency it was time to retire from Congress and move on to other things.

With limited polls and reporting on the House races it is difficult to say how the people of Ohio feel about all of these changes, but it is safe to say "confusing" is on the list.

I was disappointed to find the major party candidates so unwilling to be interviewed. However, the 3rd party candidates were very accomodating which made for some extremely interesting political discussions.

Fitrakis, Green Party Candidate for Ohio District 3
October 16, 2012

On an unusually warm Saturday afternoon in October, I met with Bob Fitrakis at the palatial home and radio studio in east Columbus the mortgage crisis had enabled him to purchase and convert to his purposes. In addition to being a Green Party candidate, Fitrakis is a politcal science professor, radio journalist, has been an election monitor in Central America, has testified before Congress about election fraud in the United States, and has worked for Republicans on the Ford Foundation, Democrats like Gerry Brown, the Democrat Socialist Party, and has now been involved with the leadership of the Green Party in Ohio for many years.

Political Philosophy

I asked Fitrakis about his myriad political associations, and if there was a common thread between them. He didn't hesitate, "Social justice…opposition to concentration of wealth…" he described his work with other parties as having been prior to

Ohio Green Party Headquarters

they had changed. The Republicans were more libertarian before being coopted by the religious right. The Democrat Socialists became subsidiaries of the Democrats. And the Democrats had become just another corporate party. He began listing off old Republicans like Eisenhower and Nixon who would "look like socialists" in today's political climate.

He described himself as a Market Socialist, believing that we should "use the profits of capitalism to take care of the workers", and is passionately opposed to the sort of "corporatism" he sees today in the bank bailouts and tax cuts for the wealthy.

On the Issues

On the Fitrakis for Congress [2] website, he lists five issues which are his top priorities, if elected. I went through the list with him. These are some of the issues most relevant to this election cycle.

1) Full Employment
This is a big point for the Green Party, included in the Green New Deal [3] being promoted by their Presidential Candidate, Dr. Jill Stein. The argument being made that if we redirect our funding priorities away from the military, foreign policy, and fossil fuel subsidies, instead supporting Domestic priories, green industry, and workers/consumers we could have full employment in America. My questions, of course, were: how? And what would it look like?

Fitrakis described a system that would have an initial cost of $592 B (less than half the price tag of the bailout), with an annual cost of $300 B thereafter. Financing to come from funds reallocated from military budget (described below), restoring Clinton era tax levels, legalizing and taxing marijuana, and a 1/10 of 1% transaction tax on speculative stocks. (a transaction tax occurs when currency changes hands, and therefore would be separate from/in addition to any unearned income tax that may exist)

Included in this cost are 24 million unemployed, twice the official number. As he points out, "one of the few things the Republicans have got right is that the numbers are wrong, because so many people have simply stopped looking and therefore aren't being reported…". According to Fitrakis, approximately 45% of this 24 million, have been out of work for 27 months or more, and a significant percentage of those are high or medium skill level.

In the Green Party Full Employement plan, those with high skill levels would receive $21/hr, medium skill levels $18/hr, and unskilled $15/hr. Of course these are national average numbers, which would vary based on locale and marketplace. The result would be lower poverty rates, lower crime rates, lower prison rates, and and an all around stronger economy.

This would not be every citizen, just those not employed in the traditional manner. What would these people be doing? Refurbishing the over 6000 abandoned homes in America and adding solar cells, thus raising property values while stimulating a green industry. Rebuilding bridges and roads, making them safe for citizens and commerce. And developing a national commuter train network between our major cities, "I believe we can have a train system at least as good as Albania and Bulgaria. Call me a crazy, wild eyed, radical, but I believe we have that capacity."

2) Rational Foreign Policy

"I actually favor the Chinese approach…" by which Fitrakis meant he prefers the idea of keeping our standing military within our borders during peacetime, and using our financial and diplomatic leverage to encourage other nations to pursue policies we prefer. He questioned the need for over 800 military bases in 160 nations, if we are surrounded by oceans and friendly nations. He did not take a completely pacifist stance, but suggested if we were engaged in foreign operations it should be under the auspices if the United Nations, or similar multi-lateral approaches. Although he does feel it is time for us to exit NATO, as it no longer serves a defensive purpose, it's enemies long gone and it's recent actions clearly offensive. "…there's a difference between arming rebels and targeting tanks every time they move."

3) Green Energy

Fitrakis fully supports the Green Party position that we should completely remove ourselves from fossil fuels and nuclear power, in favor of a completely green powered grid. Citing a Bloomberg report, he posited that the only thing standing in the way of viability is a stimulus project to kick start the industry. Suggesting that with such a project we could transition our entire society in ten years, if we just dedicate ourselves to it as we did going to the moon.

The results of such an effort, he describes, would not just be jobs and less pollution. We would also free ourselves from dependency on the utility grid, and weaken the power of the global corporations. He points to actual production of solar cells in Detroit, and solar sheeting being developed at UCLA which is 70% transparent as viable products whose cost is only out of reach because it doesn't receive the style of support that helped launch the oil industry at the beginning of the last century.

Vote for Bob?

I ended the interview by asking him why the voters of the 3rd district should cast their ballot for him, as opposed to one of the traditional parties, or the Libertarians?

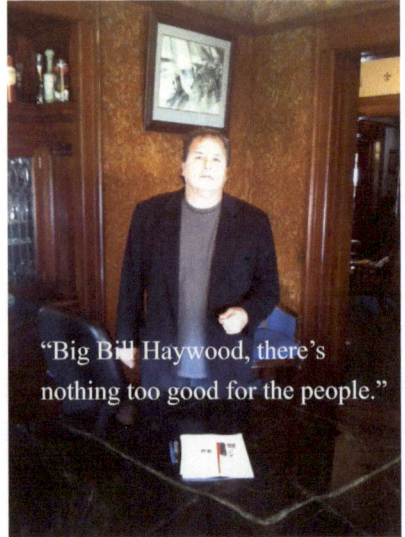

"Big Bill Haywood, there's nothing too good for the people."

"I would actually create full employment in the United States…[currently] 4% of the population locks up 1/4 of the population of the Earth, that's my definition of a police state… I would help make a better world and a safer world… I wouldn't stimulate banks, I would invest that money in local credit unions with democratically elected boards."

Whether these ideas are good, I'll leave to the reader to decide. The fact that the ideas of the "third parties" are rarely heard in any election cycle, I have to say I find offensive, as a citizen.

External Links

[1]
http://www.google.com/url?q=http%3A%2F%2Fjdadler.com%2Fbob-fitrakis-green-for-us-congress-ohio-3rd%2F&sa=D&sntz=1&usg=AFQjCNEgWKofzWQaiwMAwW97fBvO_sGNKw

[2]
http://www.google.com/url?q=http%3A%2F%2Ffitrakisforcongress.org%2F&sa=D&sntz=1&usg=AFQjCNEbxe0BFVI__Fo9K5lxHxoeOb0Gkw

[3]
http://www.google.com/url?q=http%3A%2F%2Fwww.jillstein.org%2Fgreen_new_deal&sa=D&sntz=1&usg=AFQjCNFyLDarVdH3sIeRxygBVUnsFg0g5w

Richard Ehrbar, Libertarian for Ohio's 3rd District

Oct. 15, 2012

On a warm autum day inside an overpriced
Jewish deli in the German Village section of
Columbus, Ohio, I sat down with Richard
Ehrbar, the Libertarian Candidate for US
Congress from District 3. Richard is nothing
if not passionate about the economic and
philosophic models he has clearly spent a
great deal of time studying. Neatly tucked
into a dark, polyester suit, and shaking my

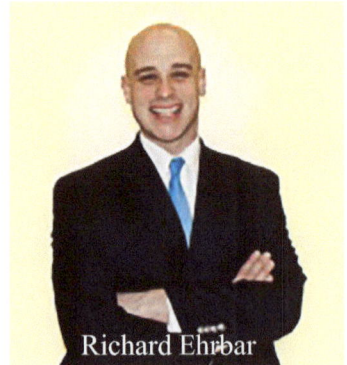

Richard Ehrbar

hand with bone breaking intensity, Richard's enthusiasm is infectious
regardless of your political positions.

Viability

We began our discussion with the simple question as to why anyone
should consider the Libertarian party, when the odds are so clearly
stacked in favor of the Democrats and Republicans. That set him off and
running with stats: "80% of the electorate say they would consider
voting for a third party if viable, Independent is the largest growing
registration with a 25% increase in Ohio, Johnson (the Libertarian
Presidential candidate) is polling at 10.6%, when mentioned,
Libertarians are on the rise among Latinos and youth, 1/3 of registered
voters don't vote". I didn't fact check this full litany of data, because the
key point here, really, is that he sees opportunity for his cause among
disaffected voters, and he is excited about it.

Military

The military policy of the Libertarians, which Ehrbar holds the line on,
is of particular significance because it affects so many other plans. First,
he wants to end all current engagements, this includes the active war in
Afgahanistan, the mission in Libya, and the drone missions in Yemen

and elsewhere. Second, a strategic review of the over 800 US bases in 160 nations worldwide to determine when, where and how we can begin reducing them.

His argument in favor of this is three fold; we finished the original mission (Bin Laden dead and Al queda/Taliban uprooted), we have no idea what the current mission is, and the endless debt liability will eventually break us just as it did the Soviets and the Romans.

I asked him if we didn't have a responsibility to finish what we started, to which he gave an impassioned, "We've been hearing that for ten years! We have to continue to break things in order to fix them. Does that make any sense? They don't want us there, just look what's happening all over that region now."

Which led to a discussion about the cause of these wars, which he defined as resource aquisition. "...oil, poppy, and what did we 'happen to stumble upon' in Afghanistan? Lithium, which powers batteries for all our computers and cell phones."

Ultimately the goal of the Libertarians for our military, after a transition phase, is to have a defensive military contained within sovereign territory and a navy that patrols open waters. This is important, not only because it is inline with their political philosophy of a government that never instigates force, but also because it is essential to their budget plans.

Domestic Security

If elected, Richard Ehrbar intends to push for repeal of the Patriot Act, to end the TSA, and to end the Drug War. As well as lobbying the President to pardon non-violent drug offenders. All of this falls under the philosophical umbrella of civil liberty; the government has no authority to interfere with you in this way, nor does the effort actually produce greater security though it does reduce freedom.

The Drug War immediately elicits a diatribe on it's overall detrimental effects; we're less safe, drain on the economy, creates a police state, we lock up more of our population than any other nation, etc. I questioned the wisdom of legalizing drugs such as heroin or meth, to which he was quick to ascribe the profitability of the black market as the driving force behind the success of those products. He suggested we look to Portugal as a model, as they have legalized drugs ten years ago and seen an overall reduction in drug use, aids, and crime.

The Patriot Act, for Libertarians, stands as a symbol of everything they oppose about current governing philosophy. It abridges Constitutional rights, regulates behavior, and uses tax dollars to force people to behave in certain ways. This, of course, lead into another discussion about the loss of freedom in America. At which point I had to stop him and ask him if he could point to specific examples of actual loss of freedom. I have to credit Ehrbar here because in this, and other cases, he is able to be specific about his ideas. A rare quality in politicians these days. His list included the following: Free Speech Zones, Arbitrary application of fines for political signs, Sections 215 and 505 of the Patriot act which allow for seizure of financial records, library records, and mail, and warrantless wire taps. Its hard to disagree with these critiques of our government as violating our rights. However, in the day to day, it's hard to say we feel any actual affects from these measures.

The TSA, airport security, is another example of where Ehrbar believes both efficiency and liberty can be better achieved through decentralization of authority. Simply by allowing the private airlines and local government to handle the job themselves.

Taxes, Banking, and the US Budget

This is where Libertarians live and breathe, and Ehrbar is no different. The IRS, the 16th Amendment, the Federal Reserve, all need to be abolished, our currency needs to be commodity based, and our budget needs to be balanced. He recognizes the need to transition from our current policies to the ideal he espouses, but is convinced that failure to do so will be devastating for our nation.

On taxation, he sees the income tax, and the 16th Amendment which authorizes it, as immoral violations of our privacy and liberty. The idea that the government can take the "first fruits" of our labor by deducting from our paychecks constitutes force and therefore is unconstitutional. Ehrbar would replace this system with purely voluntary taxes systems such as sales and excise taxes.

Which, of course, begs the question, would that raise enough funds? But one must remember that we are talking about a budget that has slashed the military in half, privatized entitlements, turned welfare over to the states, ended Obamacare, dramatically reduced foreign aid, and cut most regulatory programs. So the outlays are far less, making the need for tax revenue for less. Which also makes balancing the budget far easier. In addition, legalizing industrial hemp would create a massive increase in domestic agriculture and industrial production, particularly for Ohio where it can be grown and then used in the auto industry for both parts and fuel.

The truly revolutionary part of Ehrbar's plan would be in our banking systems. Currently the Federal Reserve is responsible for our currency and banks through a complex system of loans and interest rate adjustments. Officially their mission is twofold; to provide full employment and maintain price stability. Ehrbar judges them to be a failure at both, partly due to a lack of oversight, but also due to the inherent weakness of a fiat currency which will always decrease in value as you print more currency. As evidence he points to the fact that since 1913, when the Fed was created, the value of the dollar has decreased in value 98%, savings have decreased, and we have been at a near constant state of war due to the ability to print more money to fund them.

The alternative he offers is to transition by creating a second, commodity backed, currency. Eventually the Federal Reserve and its fiat currency system would no longer exist, replaced by local and state banks holding the commodity currency. Consumers would then be able to choose between banks based on the percentage of reserves they held. Low risk savings would mean they held reserves equal to the dollars placed in the bank by customers. High risk, and therefore high interest, would mean they held low reserves (10-20%). The perceived benefit of this system being that there would be lower inflation rates and less government expansion, due to the inability to simply print money as wanted when it is being weighed against an actual commodity.

Why Richard Ehbrar?

I asked him why the voters should choose him over the other options before them in this election.

"I am the only candidate in the 3rd district who will advocate for the elimination of unjust force."

Harlow, Libertarian for Ohio's 10th Congressional
Dayton, Ohio 10/05/12

To call Dave Harlow angry would be to call rain wet. Mr. Harlow is fed up with our 2 party political system, our failed education system, our constricting regulations, and a foreign trade policy that handicaps American business. And he has no compunction about sharing that with you. As a retired engineer, he believes he can see solutions that professional politicians and lawyers can not. Nor does he tow the Libertarian party line on all issues, diverging when he believes the best solution warrants.

Issues

On energy, he does not see green solutions as "being there yet" and therefore we need to move foreword with coal and natural gas. On several occasions he condemned the President for his "war on coal" believing it would ultimately cost him Ohio. Although he opposes the EPA on principal, he is not willing to completely abandon it, recognizing the positive influence it has had on making natural gas exploration safer, "it [the EPA] needs to be heavily curtailed"

On global warming he recognized the serious impact headed our way, but saw no method for dealing with it in a fiscally responsible manner. "people will not change until threatened."

On foreign trade and domestic industry he sees a connection. The open markets, in his opinion, with nations like China that control their currency, make it impossible to have true free trade. Although he knows this puts him at odds with other Libertarians, he recommends a period of temporary protectionism while we rebuild our industry with projects like the STEM group.

On divided government, unsurprisingly, his best recommendation is the addition of third parties. Though when asked what he could do about it if elected, he gave perhaps the most honest answer I have received from a politician, "I'm not sure I could do anything about that."

Candidacy

When asked why he was running, Harlow gave a meandering answer about originally intending to run against Boehner as he had in the prior election, but the redistricting prevented that, so he was protesting the two party system and failed policies. When asked why someone should vote for him, he laughed and gave three answers that were humorous but clearly he meant as well;

"I'm not a lawyer. I'm too old to be corrupted. Engineers are problem solvers."

While Harlow lacks the polish of a professional politician, he definitely has passion. He does not fool himself into believing that his candidacy has a chance of victory in this cycle, but he does hope to raise his issues into the public debate. Considering the level of ire on both sides of the traditional lines this election season, he just might have a chance.

Via Twitter September- November 2012

Don Lemon @donlemon
@DonLemonCNN watching this debate makes me question why more people aren't apart of the Libertarian or the Green party #MediatorLemon

Joel West @iamjoelwest
Green Party and Libertarian Party Candidates debate in US election tonight. Press gallery said to be empty

Kyle Plunkett @kyleplunkett
[ ] Democratic Party [ ] Republican Party [ ] Libertarian Party [ ] Green Party [√] Pizza Party

Rylan Strader @rylandogg
I vote by taking a shit on the ballot and the name with least amount of poop on it wins. Mostly green party/libertarian last 3 elections.

Mike Ammon @mikesmithammon
In the #3rdPartyDebate the Green Party and the Libertarian Party candidates both agree that we should stop #DroneStrikes & #StopNDAA

Brett @dza13
The only presidential candidates who support marijuana legalization are Libertarian Party Gary Johnson and Green Party Jill Stein.

Chris Chandonait @chjch
@TheSunChronicle @tscpolitics Debates should be open to the Green Party and Libertarian Party. End corporate sponsorship in politics

Jonas Wisser @jwisser
REMINDER: tonight Green Party candidate Jill Stein and Libertarian Party candidate Gary Johnson will be holding a debate via Google Hangout.

Shane Remington @roadhacker
As an American I find it infuriating that the Green, Justice and Libertarian party candidates are locked out of the Presidential Debates.

Cincinnati, Ohio
October, 2012

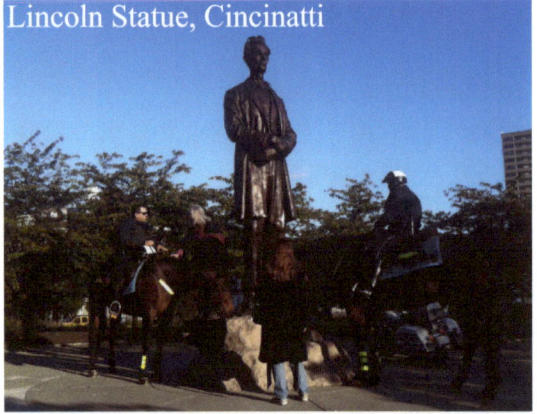
Lincoln Statue, Cincinatti

I can't wrap my head around Cincinnati. It looks like a mid-sized city, but feels like a small town. On a Sunday afternoon, the Bengals were playing, crowds walked to the stadium down the winding city walk, but when I went looking for bars in the city, I was hard pressed to find something open. Eventually, I discovered a pub that had TVs displayed like a sports pub, but was decorated like an artsy gastro-pub where one would expect to find hipsters reading bad poetry.

My couchsurf host was a young man, "Tom", who worked with software in some manner I didn't pay close enough attention to remember, which is humorous in that my interest in his work mirrored his interest in mine. His high rise apartment held a fantastic view of the city, and he provided me a taste of the city's famous Spaghetti Chili, which was tasty (even if my bowels disagreed). This was the only place I actually slept on a couch. Which is not a complaint, it was both comfy and free, which was all I asked and incredibly generous.

Tom was the only host I met who considered himself a Republican. However, he had not been following the election closely at all. Primarily because he felt he had no one to support. Obviously, President Obama was too liberal for him, but he felt Governor

west Cincinatti, Ohio

Romney couldn't be trusted and those statements Tom did believe, he didn't like. As we discussed political philosophy, he supported the individualist, laissez faire concepts, but when I pointed out specific programs (EPA, CHIP), he began by opposing the idea, but the details were always acceptable. Often when I described the history of a certain economic policy, he would concede my point.

Which is not to describe him as a hypocrite, or unintelligent, Tom was simply not a political person. When discussing his work, he demonstrated greater than average intellectual acumen. He simply had not spent significant time considering or researching political issues because they weren't of interest to him. With cursory knowledge provided in school and gleaned from media, he had formed opinions that seemed logical to him. Also, perceiving the candidates provided him by the parties were more focused on self interest than keeping promises, he saw little reason to invest a personal stake in the process. Thus, finding himself unwilling to allocate his loyalty to any side due to both philosophy and lack of trust, he had become what the pollsters would call an undecided voter. Though I think it might be more accurate to describe him as disillusioned.

east Cincinatti, Ohio

Via Twitter September - November 2012

Jonathan Mandell @newyorktheater
Will Ohio 2012 wind up like Florida 2000? #ElectionsForLawyers

Rebecca Schoenkopf @commiegirl1
Dudes, this Sherrod Brown/Josh Mandel Ohio Sen. debate is fucking
hilarious

fooler initiative @metroadlib
if josh mandel had bitches, sherrod brown would get to fuck them,
tonight. regrettably for brown, josh mandel is a homosexual.

Working America @workingamerica
Sherrod Brown: "Unlike Josh Mandel, I trust a woman to make her own
healthcare decisions." #ohdebate

NRSC @nrsc
"If you're happy the Government hasn't passed a budget in 3 years,
Sherrod Brown is your guy" - Josh Mandel #OHSen

Chemi Shalev @chemishalev
Democrat Sherrod Brown beats Jewish Republican Josh Mandel in race
that pitted pro-Israel forces against each other

Andrew Romano @andrewromano
Why did Sherrod Brown beat Josh Mandel in Ohio? Because outside
money still can't make a bad candidate good:
thedailybeast.com/newsweek/2012/…

Andy Kroll @andrewkroll
Want a clinic on dodging questions & obfuscation? Watch Ohio Senate
candidate Josh Mandel on the auto bailout: bit.ly/WNDeIY #OHSEN

Michelle @insomniac19
The Ohio senate race is a clusterfuck. Everything in Ohio right now is a
clusterfuck.

Great American Senate Race

9/01/2012

Often forgotten in the spectacle of Presidential politics is that there is an important battle for control of the US Senate going on this year as well. If either party can gain 60 seats they can control the agenda of both houses by determining what legislation is able to come to a vote in the Senate.

Likely Dem	Leans Dem	Toss Up	Leans GOP	Likely GOP
*ME: Open (R)	FL: Nelson (D)	CT: Open (D)	AZ: Open (R)	NE: Open (D)
NJ: Menendez (D)	HI: Open (D)	IN: Open (R)	NV: Heller (R)	
PA: Casey (D)	MI: Stabenow (D)	MA: Brown (R)	WI: Open (D)	
WA: Cantwell (D)	MO: McCaskill (D)	MT: Tester (D)		
WV: Manchin (D)	NM: Open (D)	ND: Open (D)		
Safe Dem Seats		OH: Brown (D)		
		VA: Open (D)		

Source: Real Clear Politics

According to Real Clear Politics [2], if the election were held tomorrow the Democrats would hold 47 seats and the Republicans 46, with 7 seats up for grabs; CT, IN, MA, MT, VA, OH, ND. If this prediction is accurate, neither side can gain the 60 seats necessary to defeat the dreaded Filibuster

Outside of this list only NV, AZ, FL, and NM appear to be mathematically in play, having spreads of less than 10%. Which is still not enough to sway the Senate one way or the other, if either side could grab them all. It is also worth noting

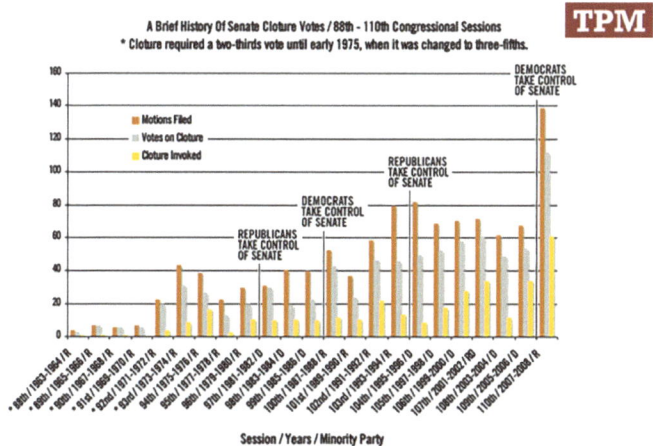

A Brief History Of Senate Cloture Votes / 88th - 110th Congressional Sessions
* Cloture required a two-thirds vote until early 1975, when it was changed to three-fifths.

Source: Talking Points Memo

that Maine, formerly Republican, will be represented by an independent in the next Senate, barring a miracle. Angus King, the Independent former Governor of the state was leading the candidates of both parties, as of June, by over 20 points. While a true political independent, King should be reliable for either side regarding breaking a filibuster.

The next legislative session will face serious debates about the tax code, the budget priorities, the debt ceiling, immigration policy, military strategy and investments, and foreign policy. If the Senate remains divided, unable to move forward on legislation, it is difficult to foresee how we can overcome these challenges.

External Links

[1]
http://www.google.com/url?q=http%3A%2F%2Fjdadler.com%2Fsenate%2F&sa=D&sntz=1&usg=AFQjCNGhlg72AIhITsu6iyi6PYKTas2rLQ

[2]
http://www.google.com/url?q=http%3A%2F%2Fwww.realclearpolitics.com%2Fpolls%2F2012%2Fsenate%2F2012_elections_senate_map.html%23safe_seats&sa=D&sntz=1&usg=AFQjCNGhQfDd7kp-o54mcspcXuQq1U4nCg

[3]
http://www.google.com/url?q=http%3A%2F%2Ftalkingpointsmemo.com%2Fdc%2Fthe-rise-of-cloture-how-gop-filibuster-threats-have-changed-the-senate&sa=D&sntz=1&usg=AFQjCNHd6ZG7zkMtfSLsh24Igu1HMGqVWA

Senate Race: Brown v Mandel
October, 2012

The election season in Ohio has not only been marked for it's importance as a swing state in the Presidential race, but also the potential influence it may have over the US Senate. Incumbent Sherrod Brown is facing a challenge from a young Republican state Treasurer named Josh Mandel in an hotly contested race for the Ohio Senate seat. For most of the early race Brown held a significant lead, but in early August Mandel closed the gap and tied up the race. However, since his pre-convention rush of momentum, Mandel's polling has begun to decline. Whether this is a temporary bump for Brown coming out of the DNC convention or a result of people getting to know Mandel is difficult to determine. However, the same polls show the Presidential race tightening in Ohio, as the Senate race widens.

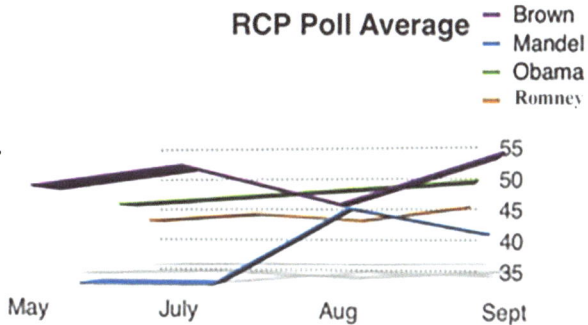

RCP Poll Average
— Brown
— Mandel
— Obama
— Romney

55
50
45
40
35

May   July   Aug   Sept

The two candidates do present significantly different visions. Where the presidential campaign lacks content, the same cannot be said for this senate race. Both campaign websites have listed several detailed points they would pursue if elected. The following is a comparison of their own words related to jobs and the economy.

Senator Sherrod Brown has dedicated a section under issues to jobs [3]. Here he outlines a traditional Keynesian plan of public investment in infrastructure and energy to stimulate growth. In a style standard to the Democrats this season, he lists programs and proposals of the past, promising of more of the same without any new proposals. In his own words:

Brown has led a fight to revitalize American manufacturing with a four-point plan, and manufacturing is on the upswing. Sherrod's four-point National

Manufacturing Strategy is based on:Innovation and Entrepreneurship –Ohio's strong history of entrepreneurship is evident in more than 30 business incubators throughout the state. Sherrod introduced the Business Incubator Promotion Act to expand eligible incubator services for support from the Economic Development Administration (EDA), and promotes economic development clusters to attract more private investment in Ohio

Education and Workforce Training –Sherrod recognized workforce systems in Ohio need to be better aligned with emerging industries that are employing more workers. In 2007, he introduced the Strengthening Economic Clusters to Organize Regional Success (SECTORS) Act, bipartisan legislation to change the way workers are trained for new jobs.

Infrastructure –Sherrod is a leader in rebuilding our decaying infrastructure. His legislation to create an Infrastructure Bank would create an innovative financing mechanism for the backlog of vital water, sewer, and road projects.

Trade Enforcement and Export Promotion –Sherrod has led the fight to give American workers and companies a level playing field, by combating China's currency manipulation and ensuring trade agreements are fair to workers. A member of the President's Export Council, Sherrod also created the Ohio Export Advisory Group to work with the Foreign Commercial Service, Small Business Administration, and Export-Import Bank in helping Ohio businesses reach new markets.

In an eleven page PDF (laid out in plaid shadow boxes), found on his website, Josh Mandel defines all of his proposals as "common sense solutions" under the umbrella of his jobs plan. Mandel supports the Conservative, Supply Side line of government austerity except for the military, low taxes, and deregulation in order to allow a free market economy to drive itself unhindered. Some excerpts from that PDF, in his own words:

Washington is broken. We need a new crop of leaders to go in and shake things up. In order to change Washington, we have to change the people we send there, and that's what this election is all about.Every two years, both Republicans and Democrats peddle so-called "jobs plans" filled with tired old federal legislation that supposedly contain the answer to our economic woes.

Both parties have failed, because their "jobs plans" are based on the false notion that politicians create jobs. The only jobs politicians create are government jobs, and we already have enough of those!Politicians can, however, help or hurt the ability of the private sector to create real jobs. That is what my plan is all about. We will develop many of the ideas in this document in greater detail on our website: jobs.joshmandel.com. But in the meantime, I want to share with you the principles that I believe will unleash the private sector economy for new job growth in Ohio and across America.

Grow the economy.The budget will not balance through spending cuts alone. It must be a balanced approach of spending cuts and economic growth.Enact a statutory spending limit.With a hard spending cap of 20% of GDP, Washington politicians would finally need to begin making the tough choices needed to get our finances under control.

Stop increasing the debt ceiling.Our goal must be to reduce the debt ceiling, not raise it. No more debt ceiling increases without real spending reform.Reexamine every regulation.Washington must sunset the federal regulations that are currently in place and reexamine each of them to ensure that they are needed, effective, and not cost prohibitive.

Scrap the tax code and start over.Move to a flatter, fairer income tax with only one or two brackets, eliminating almost all of the credits, exemptions and loopholes.

Protect small businesses.Small business is the backbone of our economy, and they must be given the opportunity to opt-out of some of the more onerous regulations.

Allow health insurance to be purchased across state lines. Increased competition among insurers will reduce prices while protecting quality.

The two theories have been competing in America for decades, each maintaining power for varying periods of time. Both parties claim their programs are designed to support job growth, small businesses, and the middle class. The natural question is, does history support either argument?

Chart 1 from the Center for American Progress [4], demonstrates that economic growth has historically accompanied higher tax rates.On the other hand, chart 2 from the NY Times [5]shows the length of various recessions since 1974, the current being the longest. We currently live in a period that possesses the lowest taxes, and the longest recession, as well as the highest government spending in years, as shown in chart 3 from usgovernmentspending. com [6].

Average annual growth in real gross domestic product, by top marginal tax rate, 1950-2010

Average real GDP growth

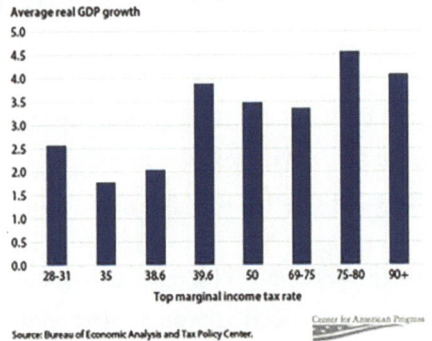

Top marginal income tax rate

Source: Bureau of Economic Analysis and Tax Policy Center.

Center for American Progress

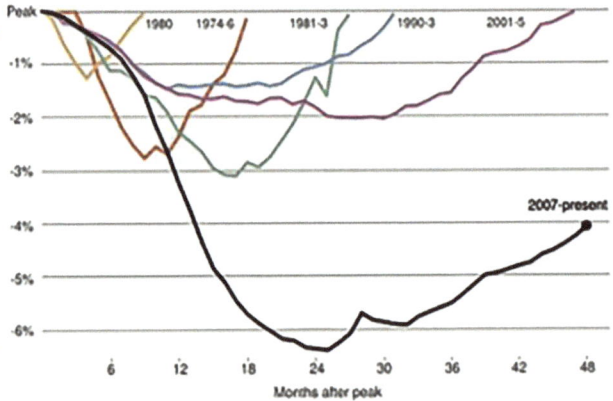

These combination of statistics suggest the possibility that any government action has little more effect on marketplace economics beyond the proverbial sweeping back of the ocean. Which still leaves the voter with the question, is it better to cut taxes and regulation so the individual can act as they see fit, or to use taxes and regulations to alleviate problems and deliver services? But if the issue of which is best for the economy is removed, as history suggests it is a wash, then the judgement becomes one of how do we wish to spend our money?A question unlikely to get the answer it deserves in a political season so filled with slogans and platitudes. Perhaps someone

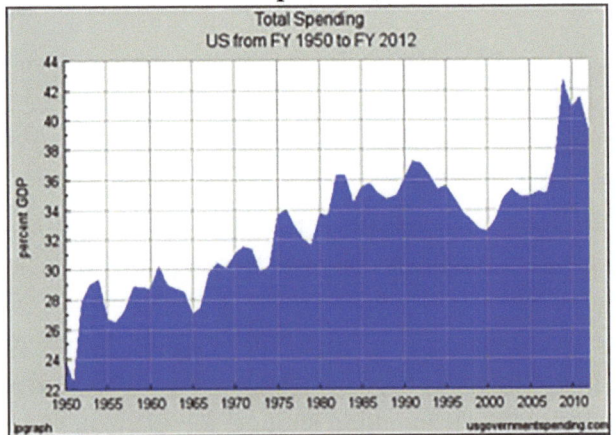

Total Spending
US from FY 1950 to FY 2012

percent GDP

usgovernmentspending.com

will develop a chart tracking the quantity of empty rhetoric to congressional inaction across US history.

External Links

[1]
http://www.google.com/url?q=http%3A%2F%2Fjdadler.com%2Fohio-senate-race%2F&sa=D&sntz=1&usg=AFQjCNGkpTEBNDOmDqb-_yt6A-pj1_aZnw

[2]
http://www.google.com/url?q=http%3A%2F%2Fwww.realclearpolitics.com%2Fepolls%2F2012%2Fsenate%2Foh%2Fohio_senate_mandel_vs_brown-2100.html%23polls&sa=D&sntz=1&usg=AFQjCNEX8z8k0mgLh-2t51OfBYhh2I0EFA

[3]
http://www.google.com/url?q=http%3A%2F%2Fwww.sherrodbrown.com%2Fissues%2Fjobs%2F&sa=D&sntz=1&usg=AFQjCNH6jcOwtKJqSdiAjPLcYouiSEUR5Q

[4]
http://www.google.com/url?q=http%3A%2F%2Fwww.americanprogress.org%2Fwp-content%2Fuploads%2F2013%2F12%2Ftrickledownecon6.pdf&sa=D&sntz=1&usg=AFQjCNGY2dRgd4UPv2vrBwkc-lVVQJqC2A

[5]
http://www.google.com/url?q=http%3A%2F%2Feconomix.blogs.nytimes.com%2F2012%2F02%2F03%2Fcomparing-recessions-and-recoveries-job-changes-4%2F&sa=D&sntz=1&usg=AFQjCNG0gVCCrsVRFMJmXXDzkFZF3WsL2Q

[6]
http://www.google.com/url?q=http%3A%2F%2Fwww.usgovernmentspending.com%2Fspending_chart_1920_2012USp_12s1li011lcn_F0t&sa=D&sntz=1&usg=AFQjCNEtv8HE7aQkD7CpD1PkoIDvbO7vug

United States Senator Sherrod Brown of Ohio, election 2012

Ohio 10/11/2012

Today I had the opportunity to speak with US Senator Sherrod Brown of Ohio for a few minutes about politics, the national debt, entitlements, green energy, and jobs as relates to Ohio.

Balanced Budget

The Senator has been a long time supporter of a Balanced Budget Amendment, but not just any amendment. In the last few years two proposals were put forward in the US Senate, one by Senator Udall(D), which he voted for, and one by Senator Hatch(R), which he voted against. He explained this dichotomy on philosophical grounds; the Udall amendment was designed to protect entitlements, while the Hatch proposal would have privatized entitlements and introduced significant tax cuts for the wealthiest Americans. A recurring theme in our discussions.

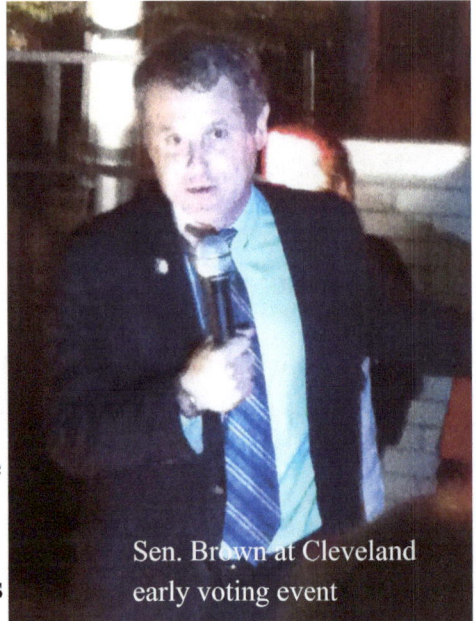

Sen. Brown at Cleveland early voting event

I asked him about Social Security in particular. While this program does not draw from the general budget, there are internal fiscal problems due to the growth in population numbers and increase in life span. Sen. Brown quickly rejected the idea of increasing the retirement age, "I don't agree with raising the retirement age… Someone working a physical job, on a factory floor…. Having them work till they're seventy…That's not a solution." When asked how he would rectify it, he pointed to the tax cap, which currently rests at the first 100,000 dollars of income, after which a citizen pays no SS taxes. "I don't know exactly what that would look like, but we don't need radical surgery… Lifting the cap [on earnings over 100,00] is the best plan."

Senator Brown's stump speeches lately have been promoting Ohio's positive growth in jobs to approximately 7.5% unemployment, ahead of the rest of the nation, along with the President's bailout of GM and the stimulus investments, as well as his own Senate jobs and education proposals such as SECTORS. He also has proposed a 5 year spending freeze, and a freeze on student loan rates at 3.4%. I asked the Senator if there wasn't a contradiction here in the desire to control debt and spending while attempting to increase spending on jobs investments. He replied with an answer that, while clearly prepared, was surprisingly salient, "We can't cut our way to prosperity….the 1960's to 1980's were some of the most prosperous times for this country, we did that through investments…we haven't invested in our infrastructure since the Reagan era…programs like Head Start and Pell Grants, lead to productive citizens…I believe in smart cuts while investing with a tax increase on our wealthiest citizens."

Open Government

Senator Brown has also been waging a battle for more open government on two fronts. In 2005, 2006, and 2011 he voted against reauthorization of the PATRIOT Act, which he sees as government overreach. I asked him if he had an opinion on what would need to happen for us to return to a pre 9/11 security footing, and he simply said, "I don't know." Not the most hopeful message, but he deserves credit for being honest in a moment where I really was expecting slogans.

He has also been a leading voice in the fight to pass a Constitutional Amendment to overturn the Citizens United decision, that essentially gave organizations the same status as individual humans. If you go to the Senator's website the first thing you find is a petition in support of such an amendment currently holding over 475 thousand signatures. (full disclosure, I am one of those signatures) The Senator was clearly angered by this issue describing it as, "…a terrible thing for democracy. It's just so cynical. To suppress voter turnout for low income voters on the one hand, while trying to buy elections on the other…It's such a cynical way to do things." He acknowledged that the amendment process was a long, slow effort, but a necessary one.

Voting Ohio

I closed the interview by asking the US Senator if he had any comments about the fight Ohio Secretary of State Husted is currently involved in regarding early voting, as Sherrod Brown once held that post for two terms. All he could say was "I'm disappointed. I thought he was going to be fair minded, try to open up elections…I think he's just thinking about his future in a party that's moving increasingly to the right."

External Links
[1]
http://www.google.com/url?q=http%3A%2F%2Fjdadler.com%2Fsen-sherrod-brown-of-ohio%2F&sa=D&sntz=1&usg=AFQjCNG5Wb4VP3_yqtSRKDdsW-FA7eHsHg

Toledo, Ohio
October, 2012

MIKE FARRELL & JAMIE FARR

A MINI-MASH REUNION JULY 12TH 2006

Made famous in the TV version of MASH by the character, Klinger, who spent the entire war trying to get sent home for wearing a dress because he was homesick for Toledo, to this day they still celebrate this fame. This is weird, not just because the show ended a couple of decades ago, but the city actually has numerous other things to offer. Although calling it a city may be hyperbolic, it's more like a small town that spread out across a city

sized territory. I consider this a compliment, as they don't suffer from the congestion or pollution of a major city, but do have most of the conveniences.

My host, John Hartman, lived in beatific residential neighborhood; tall trees and eye catching architecture in every direction. Always smiling and generous to a fault, he gave me tours of the city, meals, and a comfortable place to sleep. His home was a tchachki museum. Everywhere one looked, a collection of items could

be found that would be at home in an antique shop, 2nd hand store, or yard sale. A series of children's stories, or horror stories, could easily be set in this environ involving inanimate objects that come to life and drag the characters into a time traveling adventure.

John is what I call a disaffected liberal. His views are well within the Democrat's target audience, but he is sick of being lied to, seeing government projects fail, and the barrage of political glad-handing to which Ohioans are subjected, that he really wished would just disappear. He intended to vote for the Democrats, but only because he despised the Republicans' policies that he saw as selfish and mean spirited.

I found this to be a common meme on both sides of the aisle; opposition to the other rather than support of a leader.

Toledo Glass Museum

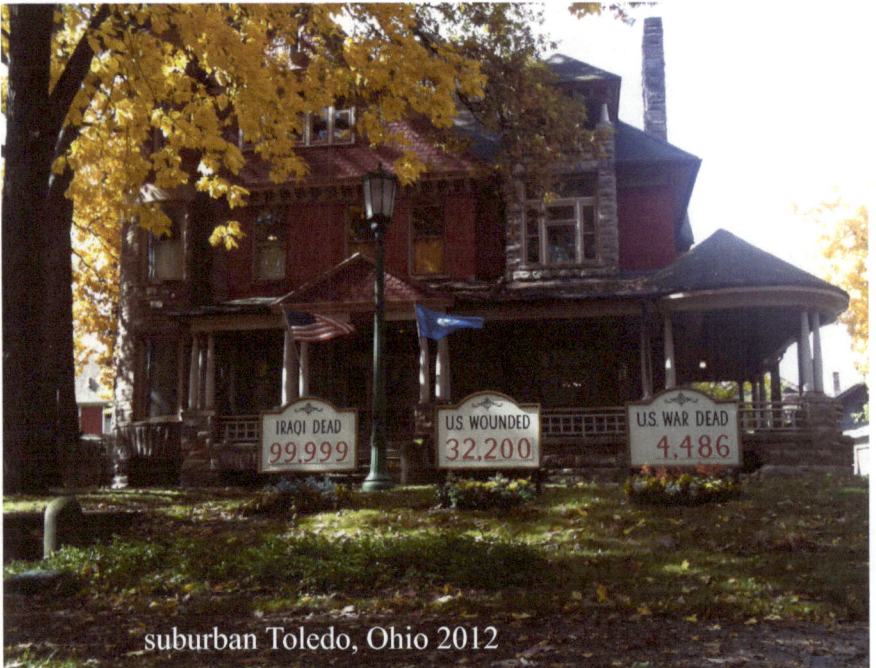

IRAQI DEAD
99,999

U.S. WOUNDED
32,200

U.S. WAR DEAD
4,486

suburban Toledo, Ohio 2012

Via Twitter September-November 2012

Right Hand Jab @lefth00k
I'M TELLING YOU: Ohio is going to have @MSNBC followers
KILLING THEMSELVES tomorrow. Barack Obama WILL NOT win
OHIO 2012 #p2 #tcot #Dayton

Geoff Ninecow @geoff9cow
Bill Clinton, Bruce Springsteen Campaign for President Obama in Ohio
2012 bit.ly/Qv7Zjw @PaddyK @GottaLaff #p2 #tcot

Gov. Gary Johnson @govgaryjohnson
10% of respondents in Gravis Marketing/Capitol Correspondent Ohio
2012 Survey would vote for @GovGaryJohnson.
race42012.com/2012/09/25/pol…

Judy Blume @judyblume
Elections have consequences. --Rachel Maddow Yes they do! Please
vote.

Donald J. Trump @realdonaldtrump
Via @digitaljournal: "Donald Trump tweets Obama is 'an incompetent
President'" bit.ly/StHskv

Yahoo @yahoo
Man who had Romney logo tattooed on face changes his mind about
keeping it: yhoo.it/YaB9vi Calls Romney "shameful," a "sore loser."

Barack Obama @barackobama
Romney now: "I like American cars." Romney in 2008: "Let Detroit go
bankrupt."

Huffington Post @huffingtonpost
Mitt Romney to Isaac flood victim who lost home: "Go home and call
211" huff.to/Q9i5ai

November 2012

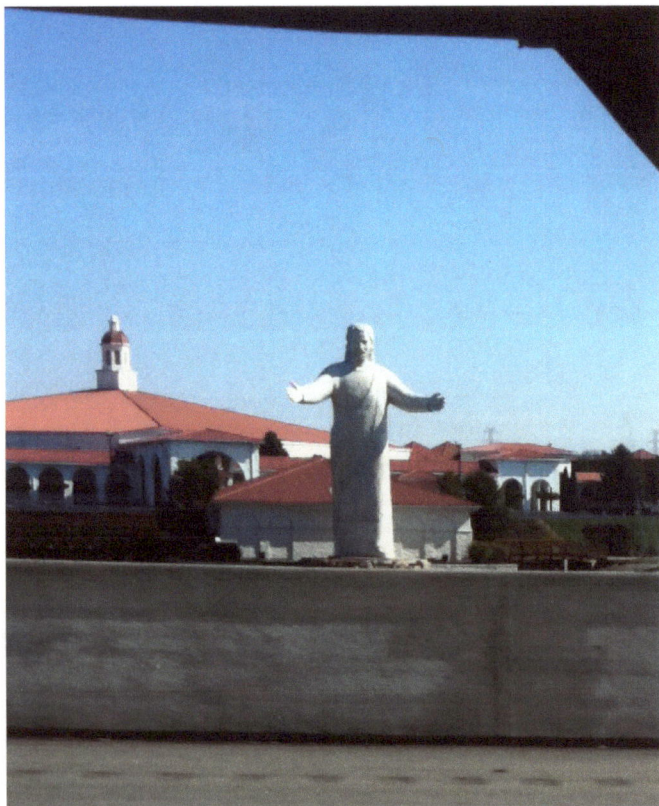

"Roadside Jesus", Ohio

Why I am Endorsing President Obama's Re-Election
Nov. 2, 2012

For 27 years I have been registered "non-partisan", like my father before me. I have voted for Democrats, Republicans, Greens, and Libertarians. I've even protest-voted for myself a few times when the only choices were between bad or worse. I don't vote based on party or slogan, I vote based on my informed belief in the ability of the candidate to accomplish both the job requirements and the goals they have laid out. This will be the first year I have ever voted a straight party ticket, and it will be Democrat.

The Republicans

I've spent the last month traveling Ohio covering down ballot races as a freelance journalist. I've also been following the various races and issues around the nation. Frankly, I am stunned and offended by the campaign the Republicans have been waging. At least six old men have argued they know what's best for the victims of rape. Many have argued that science is a hoax and faith is a more reliable method for both education and governance. They seem to believe that actions in the world can have no long term consequences, and saying otherwise must be a plot. The Republican party has shown such a disregard for the value of knowledge that they actually said, "We won't let our campaign be dictated to by fact checkers." On top of all of this, they have turned away from traditional conservative ideologies of a community of responsible individuals, to a new theory of "every man for himself, the ends justify the means".

Each of these ideas, individually, are bad enough. As a combination, representing the party's overall political ideology, they actually serve to undermine the foundations of western civilization upon which the success of America is built; Humanist ethics, Abrahamic morality, and critical thinking.

Critical Thinking and Western History

From the Renaissance through the Enlightenment and Age of Reason into the Industrial and Information Ages, western civilization has developed by confronting challenges, forming hypothesis, gathering data, either disproving or proving that hypothesis, and then moving forward; AKA the scientific method. At no time was any of this done in isolation. Each person, community, and generation builds upon the work of others to create new accomplishments of its own. There is no internet for DARPA and CERN to build without Franklin and Tesla, who in turn owe to others down the line, even to Descartes for developing the scientific method in 1637, and to Plato and Democritus for introducing critical thinking into western culture centuries before the common era. The Republican argument against science, critical thinking, and fact based debate is an argument against the development and progress of our culture.

Morality in Western Culture

The Abrahamic faiths (Judaism, Christianity, and Islam) which inform the morality of western culture, whether you subscribe to them or not they are rooted in the zeitgeist, are also undermined by this new Republican party. Despite its zealous protestations of fealty. The golden rule, "treat others as you wish them to treat you [because they will]" is the most basic precept in all world religions, but is specifically enunciated in both Judaism and Christianity. The other basic tenant of these faiths is the idea that worldly possessions are meaningless in the face of good vs evil. The argument Republicans are now making, that we should not use the tools of our government to assist each other when downtrodden, that the pursuit of cash is of greater importance than the pursuit of a better nation for us all, stands diametrically opposed to these moral values.

Humanism and the Social Contract

One of the core precepts of Humanism is the Social Contract; the idea that all living things are born free and we humans choose to sacrifice a portion of that liberty to form societies for our common benefit. That sacrifice takes the form of things like taxes, which take some of our earnings, and laws, which limit our choices, while the benefits take the form of security in food, shelter, and justice, etc. We don't ask for delivery on a silver platter, nor do we allow tyranny. The goal is to end the natural state of survival of the fittest so that we can progress to higher achievements, such as flight and curing polio. The Republicans of today are arguing that all of the progress of the last four centuries was built upon an unethical philosophy, and that we should each be left to our own devices, damn the consequences. They are arguing against Western Culture.

This is not like the Republicans of the past. This is a new, dangerous breed whose aversion to knowledge makes them unaware of the devastating outcome of their philosophy. Allowed to continue to its inevitable conclusion their lack of foresight, caustic xenophobia, brutal greed, and devout ignorance would lead Western society into a new dark ages.

The Democrats

Though President Obama and the Democrats are hardly Einstein, Keynes, or Locke, and certainly deserve criticism for their continued support of the security state, at least we can rely on them to remain invested in building upon the foundations we have been laying down for the since ancient Greece. The ideas of democracy that inform both our republic and our economy, which have allowed for an expansion of civil rights and the middle class through mass education, free speech, and economic safety nets, cannot be abandoned. The Democrats have staked their political fortunes on this mission, while the Republicans have staked their political fortunes on undermining it all. For this reason, it has never been more important to support an electoral victory for a President and his party.

Sex

Mr. Obama maintained his 2008 support among women.

	All states	N.Y.	Mass.	Calif.	N.J.	Conn.	Iowa	Wis.	Nev.	N.H.	Pa.	Va.	Fla.	Colo.	Ohio	N.C.	Ariz.	Mo.	Ind.
Male	Romney: 52%	56	55	54	55	51	53	51	49	51	51	51	52	51	52	54	54	54	57
Female	Obama: 55%	68	65	64	62	63	59	57	57	58	56	54	53	51	55	51	50	53	52

Race & Ethnicity

The white vote went to Mr. Romney, mostly by wide margins. But Hispanics and Asians moved toward Mr. Obama, continuing their consolidation as Democrats.

	All states	N.Y.	Mass.	Calif.	N.J.	Conn.	Iowa	Wis.	Nev.	N.H.	Pa.	Va.	Fla.	Colo.	Ohio	N.C.	Ariz.	Mo.	Ind.
White	Romney: 59%	49	57	53	56	51	51	51	56	51	57	61	61	54	57	68	62	65	60
Black	Obama: 93%	94	92	96	96	93	N.A.	94	92	N.A.	93	93	95	N.A.	96	96	N.A.	94	89
Hispanic	Obama: 71%	89	N.A.	72	N.A.	79	N.A.	66	71	N.A.	80	64	60	75	54	68	77	N.A.	N.A.
Asian	Obama: 73%	N.A.	N.A.	79	N.A.	N.A.	N.A.	N.A.	50	N.A.	N.A.	66	N.A.	N.A.	N.A.	N.A.	N.A.	N.A.	N.A.

Source: NYTimes

Age

Young voters favored Mr. Obama, but less so than in 2008.

	All states	N.Y.	Mass.	Calif.	N.J.	Conn.	Iowa	Wis.	Nev.	N.H.	Pa.	Va.	Fla.	Colo.	Ohio	N.C.	Ariz.	Mo.	Ind.
18-29	Obama: 60%	72	73	71	63	66	56	60	68	62	63	61	66	N.A.	63	67	66	58	49
30-44	Obama: 52%	61	56	60	59	55	52	51	54	50	55	54	52	50	51	51	56	55	49
45-64	Romney: 51%	61	59	53	60	58	52	51	49	50	51	53	52	51	51	53	56	55	56
65+	Romney: 56%	59	56	52	52	54	50	52	55	55	57	54	58	57	55	64	67	66	65

The Lonely Republican Demographic

 If you look at the <u>exit polling</u> [2] from the election, of which there is plenty, there is only one demographic the Republican party won outright. Who is this key Republican character? He is a straight, white man over the age of 45, married, earning more than $40,000 per year, often possessing a bachelor's degree, and living in either a rural or suburban community, probably in the south or midwest. Any other demographic you could name, the Democrats won their support.

It can not be said the Republicans have not attempted outreach to other groups. They have a variety of candidates, show up at the NAACP, and they even made their convention into "night of a thousand tokens". While the presentation of their message is clearly a problem, that is not the core issue, as everyone has always believed their politicians were lying, corrupt, cynics. The reason their following is shrinking, is they are clinging to outdated philosophies.

I am reminded of my Uncle, a staunch 70-something liberal who grew up when McCarthy was purging the Jewish, Liberal, Pinko Commies out of Hollywood and Universities. We were talking politics one night and I happened to mention that one of his ideas reminded me of something in the Communist Manifesto. He was furious and offended. Merely bringing up the subject of communism caused him to stop seeing me as his nephew quoting philosophy, but rather brought him back to the battle lines of his youth. For me, it was confusing, because I did not invest such emotion in these key words of his generation, like communism.

For the Republicans who have long fought for the Pro-life, anti-socialist, anti-immigrant, low tax message, I suspect it is equally difficult to break with their paradigm just because the next generation has moved on. Which is the real problem for the Republican party. If the leadership changes their message, they risk losing these voters to some third party. If they don't change their message, they risk no longer having voters in 40 years or so.

They could change their immigration policy, and temper their socialist jingoism without losing most of their base. But if they alter course on abortion, how can the religious right stay with them and maintain their expressed values? And if they change on their tax stance, who are they?

It is highly probable that there will no longer be a Republican Party ten years from now, unless they simply keep the same name on a completely new message.

External Links
[2]
http://www.google.com/url?q=http%3A%2F%2Felections.nytimes.com%2F2012%2Fresults%2Fpresident%2Fexit-polls&sa=D&sntz=1&usg=AFQjCNHYskvgDVuZKRaNF5T7aCP3RlXuRA

The Green Party, America's Political Future?
November 12, 2012

Although not well covered, the Green Party actually had a good day on Nov. 6, 2012. While everyone else was watching the Presidential race, the Greens quietly won over thirty local races across the nation, including a state representative in Arkansas, Fred Smith, and Mayoral victories in NY and CA. This brings their total number of seats held to 140 in 25 states including 6 Mayors and 1 state representative.

The Libertarian Party appears to have gained no new seats, though they did secure enough votes to remain on the ballot in several states, next cycle. They currently hold 154 offices around the nation, including 8 Mayoralties. As to why one third party had a better showing than the other, I would hypothesize it is the same reason as the outcome of Obama v Romney; American philosophy has moved in a more liberal direction. This is where opportunity lies for the Greens, if they can figure out how to take advantage of it.

The political analysis of the last week has focused on the exit polling breakdown of ethnicity. However, Republicans didn't lose because of ethnicity on any score, they lost because the majority of the nation embraces progressive values and policies. So, when they push social policies of zero tolerance, they offend the majority. When they push economic policies based on supporting business, rather than the individual, they offend the majority. But they can't just walk away from their core values in an effort to rebrand, either, because such a cynical move would cost them their base while failing to pick up new members.

For this reason it is entirely possible the Republicans become further marginalized on the right, probably adjusting their immigration policy in a blatant pander to Hispanics. As a result the Democrats will become even more centrist in an opportunistic move to pick up moderate Republican votes. Thus the progressive move of the electorate actually pushes the government further to the right. Which leaves room on the left for a new party to represent those liberals who are becoming increasingly under-represented.

Environmentalists, Unions, Teachers, and Farmers, are all examples of traditional Democrat supporters who have felt neglected or taken for granted in recent years, and with good reason. As Democrats have fought for the growing voting blocks of independents, women, homosexuals, and youth, they have not been focusing on those groups who they believe have no alternative. The Hispanic community also has not pledged itself to any party as of yet, voting against Romney more than in favor of Obama.

The Green New Deal with its message of ending the drug war, shrinking the military, North American work visas, and having a more progressive tax code so that we can prioritize our spending towards education, agriculture, infrastructure, and alternative energy should be appealing to this Liberal base, the youth vote, and a significant portion of the Hispanic vote, based on polling. So the real challenge for the Greens is getting their voice heard. This is, of course, a Catch 22, because the media won't take them seriously until they get elected to federal office, and they can't elected to federal office without media attention, which costs money that is difficult to raise unless you already hold either office or media attention.

If they Green's wish to overcome this obstacle they need to learn the lessons of the two most successful grassroots campaigns in recent years; The Tea Party and the Obama campaign. The President won through community organizing, finding his base, and getting people to turn out and vote. The Tea Party was able to make itself heard by targeting a few favorable districts, and focusing all of their national resources there in order to get themselves national attention. Both of these groups used communications technology and in person conversations to get their message to as many people as possible.

The Green Party has built themselves a respectable national network, with numerous local office holders in several key states; CA, MA, PA, and WI. If they would forgo the Presidential campaigns until 2020, and spend the next three federal campaigns utilizing national resources to succeed in a few races, first in those four states and then expand, they stand a better chance of success. If they can win one federal office, the media will start covering them. If they win in more than one election cycle, the media will start taking them seriously. At which point they will be able to run nationwide, seriously.

Their political positions are ahead of the public opinion. Which is good for longevity and leadership. They have a network in place. They have an opportunity presented by a disorganized and out of touch Republican Party and a centrist Democrat Party ignoring its liberal base. The question remains will the Green Party be able to manage the organization and strategy necessary to take advantage of this opportunity?

2 Years Later

As we look into another election cycle for a US Congress that has achieved less than any other in history, politcal wonks project as many as 17 House seats and 9 Senate seats up for grabs. Which means the House will remain in Republican Party control regardless of the results but the Senate could switch from Democrat to Republican control if they can gain just 5 seats. However, they will never gain enough for a veto override, so the next two years will likely continue seeing a government unable to achieve anything. The only difference, it will be the President blocking Congress's agenda instead of the reverse.

One has to wonder how the America people will react after 6 years of failed government where politicians spend billions of dollars to get elected so they can do nothing other than bicker like spoiled children.

www.ingramcontent.com/pod-product-compliance
Lightning Source LLC
Chambersburg PA
CBHW040129270326
41928CB00001B/6